HOUGHTON MIFFLIN

WE·THE
PEOPLE

Work Together

WE·THE PEOPLE

Work Together

Sarah Bednarz

Catherine Clinton

Michael Hartoonian

Arthur Hernandez

Patricia L. Marshall

Pat Nickell

CARL MOORE

bee Island, on the border of South Carolina and Georgia

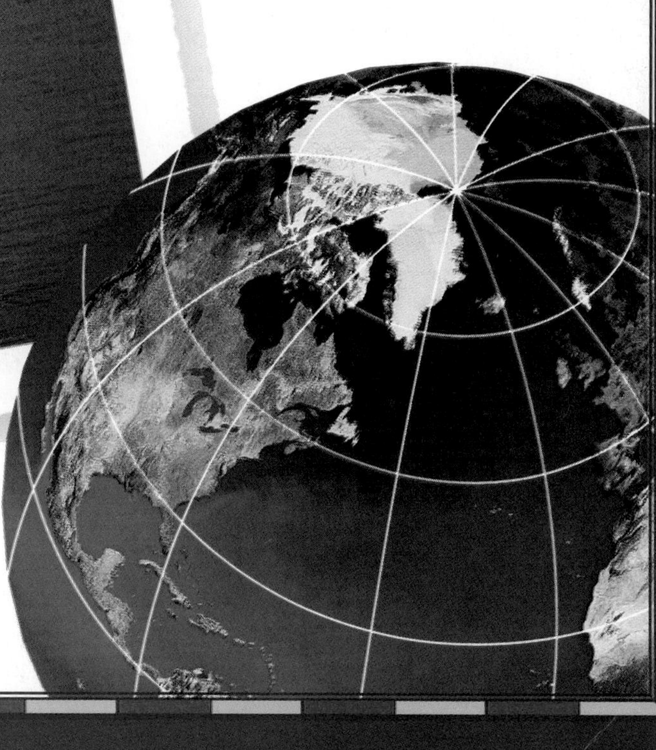

HOUGHTON MIFFLIN • Boston
Atlanta • Dallas • Denver • Geneva, Illinois • Palo Alto • Princeton

Sarah Bednarz
Assistant Professor
Texas A&M University
College Station, TX

Arthur Hernandez
Associate Professor
Division of Education
College of Social and
Behavioral Sciences
University of Texas at
San Antonio
San Antonio, TX

Catherine Clinton
Gilder-Lehrman Institute
Affiliate
Yale University
New Haven, CT

Patricia L. Marshall
Associate Professor
Department of Curric-
ulum and Instruction
College of Education
and Psychology
North Carolina State
University
Raleigh, NC

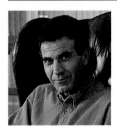

Michael Hartoonian
Professor and Director
Center for Economic
Education
University of Minnesota
Minneapolis, MN

Pat Nickell
College of Education
University of Georgia
Athens, GA

Susan Buckley General Editor

Acknowledgments appear on page 244.
2003 Impression
Copyright © 2000 by Houghton Mifflin Company. All rights reserved.

Printed in the U.S.A. ISBN: 0-618-00410-6   56789-VH-03 02

CONSULTANTS

Felix D. Almárez, Jr.
Department of History
University of Texas
San Antonio, TX

Manley A. Begay, Jr.
John F. Kennedy School
of Government
Harvard University
Cambridge, MA

William Brinner
University of California
Berkeley, CA

Phap Dam
Director of World
Languages
Dallas ISD
Dallas, TX

Philip J. Deloria
Department of History
University of Colorado
Boulder, CO

Jorge I. Domínguez
The Center for
International Affairs
Harvard University
Cambridge, MA

Sherry L. Field
Department of Social
Science Education
University of Georgia
Athens, GA

Stephen Fugita
Department of
Psychology
Santa Clara University
Santa Clara, CA

Kenneth Hamilton
Department of History
Southern Methodist
University
Dallas, TX

Charles Haynes
Freedom Forum First
Amendment Center
Arlington, VA

Tyrone C. Howard
College of Education
Ohio State University
Columbus, OH

Shabbir Mansuri
Founding Director
Council on Islamic
Education
Susan Douglass
CIE Affiliated Scholar

Dahia Ibo Shabaka
Director of Social Studies
Detroit Public Schools
Detroit, MI

Ken Tanaka
Institute of Buddhist
Studies
Graduate Theological
Union
Berkeley, CA

Cliff Trafzer
Department of History
and Ethnic Studies
University of California,
Riverside
Riverside, CA

Frank de Varona
College of Education
Florida International
University
Miami, FL

Ling-chi Wang
Department of Asian
American Studies
University of California
Berkeley, CA

TEACHER REVIEWERS

Kindergarten/Grade 1: Wayne Gable, Langford Elementary, Austin ISD, TX • **Donna LaRoche,** Winn Brook School, Belmont Public Schools, MA • **Gerri Morris,** Hanley Elementary School, Memphis City Schools, TN • **Eddi Porter,** College Hill Elementary, Wichita SD, KS • **Jackie Day Rogers,** Emerson Elementary, Houston ISD, TX • **Debra Rubin,** John Moffet Elementary, Philadelphia SD, PA

Grade 2: Rebecca Black, Sanders Elementary School, Jefferson County SD, KY • **Anne Cochran,** Centennial Elementary School, Pasco County SD, FL • **Stacy Colhouer,** Avondale West Elementary School, Topeka City Schools— USD 501, KS • **Sheila Hamilton,** Haywood Elementary School, Metropolitan Nashville SD, TN • **Kathy Headley,** School of Education, Clemson University, SC • **Nan Nelson,** Glenville School, Greenwich SD, CT • **Patricia Smith,** Language Arts/Elementary Coordinator, Sumter SD Two, SC • **Linda Thomas,** Desert Canyon School, Scottsdale SD, AZ

Grade 3: Judy Cannizzarro, Social Studies Coordinator K-12, Metro/Nashville Public Schools, TN • **Darcy Cleek,** Chester. W. Taylor Elementary, Pasco County SD, FL • **Stacy Colhouer,** Avondale West Elementary, Topeka City Schools—USD 501, KS • **Shirley Frank,** Instructional Specialist, Winston-Salem/Forsyth County Schools, NC • **Kathy Headley,** School of Education, Clemson University, SC • **Paige Krupilski,** Sanders Elementary, Jefferson County SD, KY • **Elaine Mattson,** Aloha Park Elementary,

Beaverton SD, OR • **Patricia Smith,** Language Arts/Elementary Coordinator, Sumter SD Two, SC • **Kristi Theurer,** Deer Park Elementary, Pasco SD, FL • **Irma Torres,** Galindo Elementary, Austin ISD, TX • **Paul Tune,** Sanders Elementary, Pasco County, FL

Grade 4: Lenora Barnes, Duncan Elementary, Lake County SD, IN • **Dianna Deal,** Park Hill Elementary, North Little Rock SD, AR • **Becky Murphy,** Butler Elementary, Springfield SD, IL •**Sumner Price,** Legion Park Elementary, Las Vegas City SD, NM • **Jim Wilkerson,** Glenoaks Elementary School, Northside ISD, TX

Grade 5: Pat Carney-Dalton, Lower Salford Elementary School, Souderton SD, PA • **Janice Hunt,** Dearborn Park Elementary, Seattle Public Schools, WA • **Debbie Ruppell,** Dover Elementary, Dover Union Free SD, NY • **Jon Springer,** Bethany Elementary, Beaverton SD, OR • **Nancy Watson,** Weeks Elementary, Kansas City SD, MO • **Gloria Wilson,** Forest Park Elementary, Little Rock SD, AR

Grade 6: Marcia Baynes, The Longfellow School, Middlesex County Schools, MA • **Diane Bloom,** Steelman School, Eatontown SD, NJ • **Hillary Callahan,** Coordinator of Language Arts, Roanoke City Schools, VA • **Tom Murphy,** Carusi Elementary, Cherry Hill SD, NJ • **Mark Newhouse,** A.T. Morrow School, Central Islip SD, NY • **Dot Scott,** Meadow Creek Elementary, Hurst-Euless-Bedford ISD, TX

CONTENTS

Theme 1 People and Communities

Key

city

suburb

highway

road

Theme 2 Our Place on Earth

Theme 3 People at Work

Theme 4 Our Nation's Story

Theme 5 America's People

Theme **6** Our Government

FEATURES

★ CITIZENSHIP ★

THINK LIKE A GEOGRAPHER

MAPS

Let's Explore
Map Skills

Let's Find Out
Research Skills

Let's Look
Visual Skills

LITERATURE

THEN & NOW

American Voices

We work together in our homes, in our schools, in our neighborhoods, and in our play.

We live together in communities—
small towns, big cities, and
wide open spaces.
We share a beautiful country!

We are one nation, one community—
of many cultures, of many ages.
We care about our families,
our friends, our country, our world.

We explore changes together in our communities, for today and for all our tomorrows!

"This land is your land, this land is my land. . ."

We are the

spirit of America!

People and Communities

The house I live in,
A plot of earth, a street,
The grocer and the butcher
Or the people that I meet . . .
The town I live in
The street, the house, the room,
The pavement of the city,
Or a garden all in bloom.

from the song "The House I Live In," words by Lewis Allan

Key Words

group

Lesson 1, page 10

rule

Lesson 1, page 11

neighborhood

Lesson 2, page 17

urban

Lesson 3, page 22

suburb

Lesson 4, page 28

rural

Lesson 5, page 34

Families and Friends

Main Idea We are members of groups at home, at school, and with friends.

You are a member of many groups. A **group** is a number of people who live, work, or spend time together.

A family is one kind of group. Family members work together to help each other. Your class is a group of students. Every day you work and learn together. A group of friends can read books, play games, and work together on projects.

Geography Club

In your class, you follow rules. A **rule** tells what people may or may not do. Rules help groups get along. Your class may have a rule about taking turns. What rules do you have at home?

This social studies book is about groups of people. **Social studies** looks at how and where groups of people live today and long ago.

What Did You Learn?

 Key Words: Define the words **group** and **rule**.

2 What groups are you a member of this year?

Using a Textbook

This social studies book has themes and lessons. Each theme is about a big social studies idea. The lessons help you learn more about the theme. Each lesson has many parts.

The parts are the same in every lesson. The titles, Main Idea, Key Words, and What Did You Learn? parts can help you remember and think about what you have read.

① Here's How

Look at the picture of the book on page 13.

- Look for the list of Key Words. Where can you find the list?

- Look for the Main Idea. Is it at the beginning or at the end of the lesson?

- Find the title. What is the lesson called?

The Key Words are important words to learn in the lesson.

A title tells what the lesson is about.

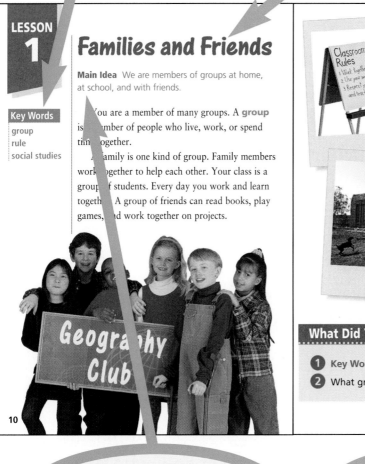

LESSON 1

Families and Friends

Main Idea We are members of groups at home, at school, and with friends.

Key Words
group
rule
social studies

You are a member of many groups. A **group** is a number of people who live, work, or spend time together.

A family is one kind of group. Family members work together to help each other. Your class is a group of students. Every day you work and learn together. A group of friends can read books, play games, and work together on projects.

10

In your class, you follow rules. A **rule** tells what people may or may not do. Rules help groups get along. Your class may have a rule about taking turns. What rules do you have at home?

This social studies book is about groups of people. **Social studies** looks at how and where groups of people live today and long ago.

What Did You Learn?

1. Key Words: Define the words **group** and **rule**.
2. What groups are you a member of this year?

11

A **Main Idea** is the most important idea in the lesson.

What Did You Learn? has questions and activities.

2 Use the Skill

Look at the parts of the lesson above.

1. What is one Key Word of the lesson?

2. What is the Main Idea?

3. In what part of the lesson would you find questions and activities about the lesson?

★ CITIZENSHIP ★

Helping Out

Have you ever helped a friend with a job? You help out, or participate, when you share work with others. Helping others makes you feel good.

Volunteers Build Houses

Megan and her family needed a new home. A group called *Habitat for Humanity* helped Megan and her family build a new house. The people who work for this group are volunteers. **Volunteers** are people who help others without getting paid.

The volunteers were not all builders. Many of them had other kinds of jobs. Some of them were teachers and police officers. They all wanted to help their neighbors.

Even children helped. Megan says, "I helped, too. I put siding on our house and painted my closet." What job would you choose?

You Take Action

1 List ideas that your class could do to help your school or community.

2 Ask your teacher to help you set up the project. Begin your project.

3 Write about your project in a one-page *Helping Hands Newsletter.* Give out copies so that the whole school can learn how you helped out.

★ Tips for Helping Out ★

- Choose a project that will help make your school or community a better place.

- List ways that each person can help out in the project.

LESSON 2

Our Communities

Main Idea People live, work, and play together in a community.

Families and friends live in many different kinds of communities. A **community** is a place where people live, work, and play together. A community has leaders who make rules.

The rules of a community are called laws. A **law** helps people in a community live together peacefully. Some laws help keep people safe. Other laws help keep the community clean.

A neighborhood is a smaller part of a community.

A community can have different neighborhoods. Your **neighborhood** is the area around your home. The people in your neighborhood are your neighbors.

Many people are proud to know and help their neighbors. They want their neighborhood to be a nice place to live. How do you help take care of your neighborhood?

What Did You Learn?

 Key Words: Use these words in sentences to show their meaning: **community, law, neighborhood**.

 What laws of your community do you know?

17

Reading a Map

A map is a drawing of a place. Maps give you information. They show where places are. They show how far places are from each other.

A compass rose shows directions on a map. The directions are North, South, East, and West. Intermediate, or in-between, directions are Northeast, Southeast, Northwest, and Southwest.

A map key is a list of the symbols used on a map. The symbols can be pictures, shapes, or colors. They stand for real things.

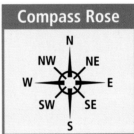

Compass Rose

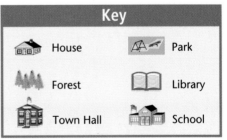

Key

House   Park

Forest   Library

Town Hall   School

① Here's How

Look at the map key.

- What does this symbol stand for?
- What symbol shows a park?

Look at the compass rose.

- What direction does SE show?

18

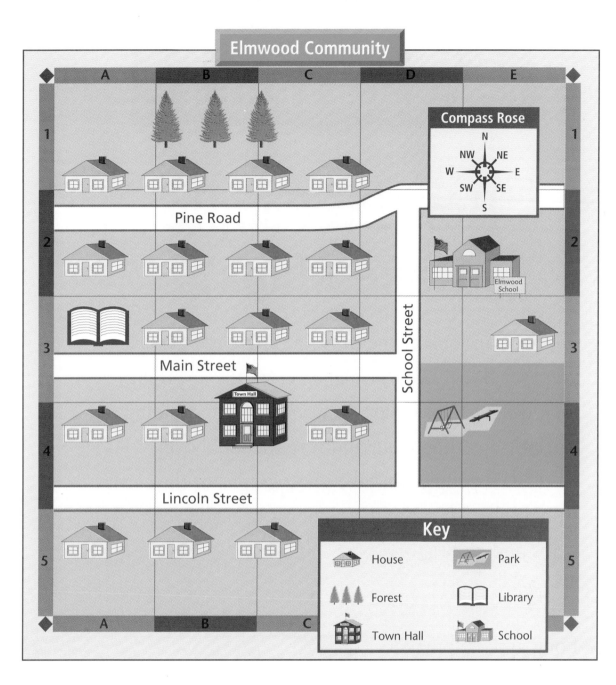

Elmwood Community

Pine Road

Main Street

Lincoln Street

School Street

Compass Rose

Elmwood School

Town Hall

Key

🏠 House   🛝 Park

🌲 Forest   📖 Library

🏛 Town Hall   🏫 School

❷ Use the Skill

1. On which street is the library?

2. In which direction would you walk from the park to the school?

3. Tell or write how to go from Town Hall to the school. Use street names and directions to help a friend find the way.

How Do People Make Maps?

You can look at the earth in different ways. Have you ever flown in an airplane? From the air, things look different than they do when you are standing on earth. Maps show land and water from above.

Today, people can take photographs of the earth from space. They use these photos to make very exact maps and globes.

Math Connection

Long ago, mapmakers could not see the world from above. They went from place to place and measured the distances. Then  they made maps based on what they measured and saw. Would you use the same tools to measure your classroom and your community?

20

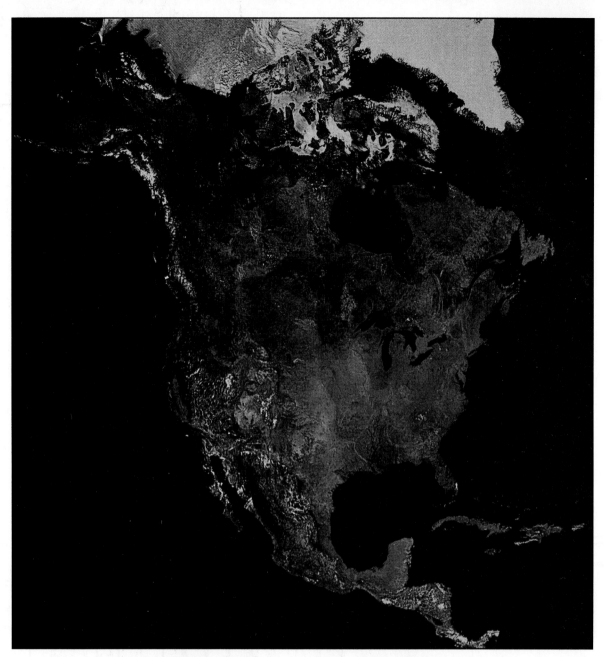

This is a photo of North America taken from space.

Think About It!

1. Look at the photo. How is this photo different from a map of North America?

2. Make a map of your classroom. Draw a picture of what it looks like from above.

Living in Cities

Main Idea An urban community has many people and many places where people can work and play.

Cars honk. Many people cross the street. Subway trains rumble underneath. You are in a city. A **city** is a community where many people live and work close together.

Cities, or **urban** communities, are full of people. They work, go to school, and come to visit. Families live close to each other in apartment buildings or houses.

There are many apartment buildings in cities.

Exploring a City

Cities are busy places. Many people move to cities to find jobs. Cities often have tall buildings that are places for people to work. Some cities can have subways and buses. Some cities are large and have many different neighborhoods. Smaller cities have only a few neighborhoods.

Some cities have skyscrapers.

Chinatown is one neighborhood in New York City.

New York is a very big city. It has many buildings, offices, stores, and schools. New York City has many neighborhoods. People within a neighborhood sometimes speak the same language and share interests.

A City on a River

Many cities are built near water. People use the water for drinking. They also use the water near a city for transportation. **Transportation** means moving things or people from one place to another. People use the land around the city for transportation too.

A steamboat is one kind of transportation in St. Louis, Missouri.

St. Louis, Missouri

Mississippi R.

St. Louis

UNITED STATES

Key
★ St. Louis
— river
+++ railroad

Trains stopped in St. Louis on their way west.

The city of St. Louis, Missouri, was built on the Mississippi River. The river has been important to the people in St. Louis. Long ago people moved in and out of the city in boats on the river. Today, people can reach St. Louis by boat, train, car, bus, or airplane.

24

City Life

Cities have many interesting places to visit. Most cities have stores, parks, and places to eat. In some cities, you can go to museums, zoos, and sports centers. Cities also have many schools for the people who live there.

Some people love a busy urban community. What other kinds of communities are there? Read on to find out!

There is a firefighters' museum in Oklahoma City, Oklahoma.

What Did You Learn?

1 **Key Words:** Describe a **city** using the words **urban** and **transportation**.

2 Where was St. Louis built?

3 Write or tell a story about a city. Tell about the people, buildings, or transportation in the city.

Communities Change

How did your community look long ago? You can find out by reading a book or using the Internet. You can learn about the buildings people made, the clothes they wore, and ways they moved from place to place.

Rome is a very old city in Italy. It is thousands of years old. Take a look at how Rome has changed.

Then

Long ago in Rome, large buildings were made of marble, stone, brick, and concrete. People came from far away to visit Rome. They came by sea, foot, or cart.

Large crowds came to the Colosseum to see sporting events.

Now Today, tourists come by car, train, and airplane to visit Rome. They visit the very old buildings there. People who live in Rome work in newer buildings made of steel and glass.

New streets and buildings crowd around the very old Colosseum.

Think About It!

1 What buildings in your community have been there for many years?

2 **Think About the Future** How do you think your community will change in the future? How will it stay the same? Draw a picture of your community in the future.

Living in the Suburbs

Main Idea Suburbs are communities outside cities.

Key Word

suburb

It's the end of the day. Tired workers get on a train in the city. As the train leaves the city, they look out the window. Buildings become smaller and farther apart. These workers are going home to communities called suburbs. A **suburb** is a community outside a city. Suburbs usually have fewer people and more open space than cities.

Explore the Suburbs

Trains and roads connect suburbs to cities. People often have to drive to work, stores, and school. Like cities, suburbs have neighborhoods. They have stores, schools, and places where people work. There is more open space for houses, yards, and parks.

Daniela's Suburb

Daniela Perez lives in a suburb of Cincinnati, Ohio. Her community is called Anderson Township. Daniela explains, "I moved here from Caracas, Venezuela (Cah RAH cahs, Vehn eh zoo EH lah). In Caracas, I lived in an apartment building in the city. Now I live in a house with a big front yard. Near my house, there are woods and a playground."

Daniela's family drives to the store to shop. They all walk to the park nearby to play. They spend most of their time in the suburb of Anderson Township.

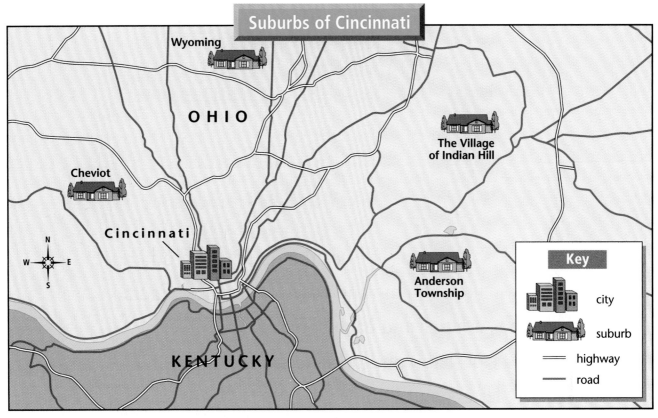

Suburbs of Cincinnati

Wyoming

OHIO

The Village
of Indian Hill

Cheviot

Cincinnati

N
W   E
S

Anderson
Township

Key

city

suburb

highway

road

KENTUCKY

Anderson Township is one suburb of Cincinnati.

In the United States, many suburbs have grown and changed. As cities grow, people build new suburbs close by. These suburbs grow when people build new houses, stores, and businesses. Are there any suburbs near you?

What Did You Learn?

 Key Words: Use **suburb** in a sentence to show its meaning.

 Compare the suburb of Anderson Township to your community.

31

Using a Map Grid

A grid is a pattern of lines that cross each other. The lines make columns and rows of squares. Each column has a letter and each row has a number.

A grid can help you find places and things on a map. The letters and numbers name each square. You can use a square's name, or address, to tell someone where something is. Or you can use a square's address to find a place on the map.

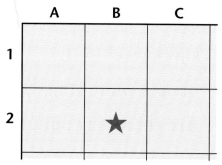

1 Here's How

Look at this grid.

- Put your finger on the star. Move it straight up to the top of the column. What is this letter?

- Put your finger on the star again. Move it sideways to the beginning of the row. What is this number?

- What is the address of the star?

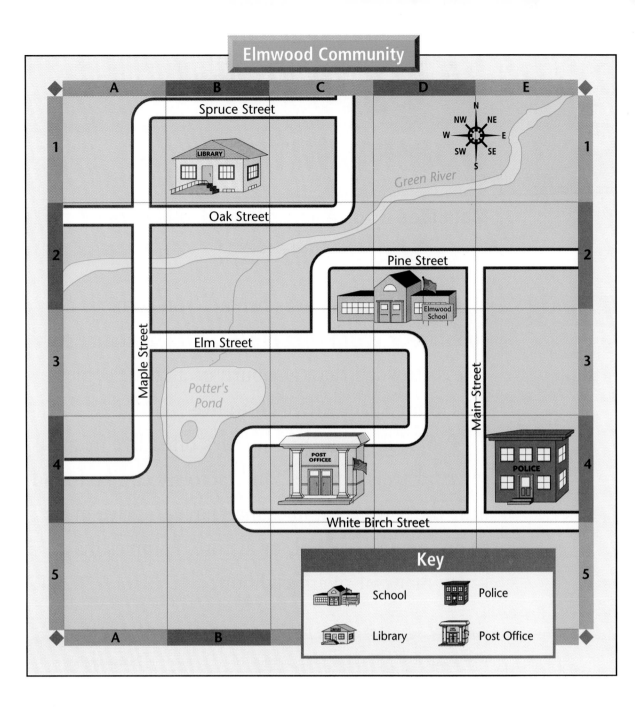

Elmwood Community

2 Use the Skill

1. Where is the Post Office? Name the square.

2. Where is the Library? Name the square.

3. What is at E4?

33

Living in Rural Communities

Main Idea People in rural communities live in small towns or in the countryside.

Key Words
rural
agriculture

Leaving the suburbs behind, you come to a country, or **rural** community. A rural community is less crowded than a suburb or a city. People have more space in which to live.

People in rural communities often live in small towns. Farms, ranches, and factories can be found near the towns. Families may have to drive miles to go to work, school, or a store. Families may know many of their neighbors.

Unity, Oregon, is a small, rural town. Most people know everyone in town. They help each other out. Some people work in town at the school or in stores.

Many people in Unity work on the land. They make their living in agriculture. **Agriculture** means raising plants or animals to sell. Some people work cutting down the trees in the area. Others work at the sawmill and turn the wood into boards for houses and furniture.

What Did You Learn?

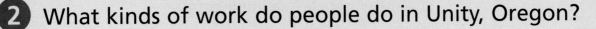

1 **Key Words:** Tell a friend about life in a small town using the words **rural** and **agriculture**.

2 What kinds of work do people do in Unity, Oregon?

Our Block

by Lois Lenski

Our block is a nice one,
    The best in town;
On each side row houses
    With steps coming down.

Our block is noisy,
    We yell and shout —
Women at the windows,
    Children running out.

Our block has music —
    Even a band!
We give a block party,
    It sure is grand!

We hang up flags
    And bunting too;
We dance to the music
    All night through.

We dance till morning,
    And then we rest;
Our block is a nice one —
    The very best.

The Best Block

Response Activity

Write a poem about your own block.
Write about the streets, homes, and land
people would see if they visited your
neighborhood.

Theme 1 Big Ideas

1. Write or draw something that you have learned about each kind of community below.

class

urban

suburb

rural

Review What You Learned

2. What are some groups that you are a part of at home or at school?

3. What are some things people can do in a city?

4. What is a suburb?

5. What is life like for families who live in rural communities?

Key Words

Use the Key Words below to fill in the sentences.

group (p. 10)   **rural** (p. 34)

neighborhood (p. 17)   **suburb** (p. 28)

rule (p. 11)   **urban** (p. 22)

6. Many people live and work close together in large _____ communities.

7. A _____ tells what you may or may not do.

8. A _____ is a community that is outside a city.

9. You can work and play with a _____ of friends at school.

10. Your _____ is the part of your community where you live.

11. Many people in a _____ community work on the land or in agriculture.

Write About Your Community

12. Make a travel guide for your community. Tell other people why they should visit. Answer these questions as you write.

   • What does your community look like?

   • Is it a suburb, or an urban or rural community?

   • What kind of groups are in your community?

   • What do you like about living in your community?

Great hiking in Denver. Visit soon!

13. What part of the lesson tells you the important words to learn?

14. What does a lesson title tell you about a lesson?

15. What does the Main Idea tell you about a lesson?

Use the map below to answer the questions.

16. What is the symbol for forest?

17. What is north of the Nature Center?

18. In what square can you find the turtles?

19. What is at A1?

20. Give the address for the parking lot.

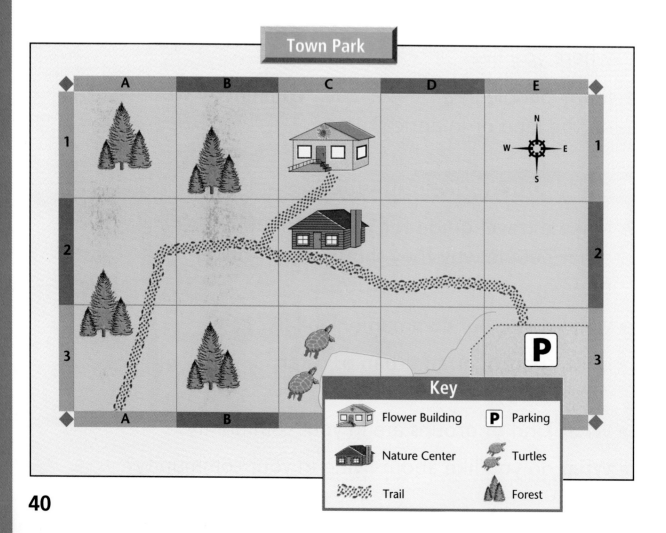

Town Park

Key

Flower Building
P Parking
Nature Center
Turtles
Trail
Forest

Make a Community Big Book

Things You'll Need
- oak tag
- large white paper
- crayons or markers
- stapler or hole punch and yarn

1 Use a few sheets of large paper. On each sheet, draw a part of your community. Your drawings should answer these questions:
- Who lives there?
- What kinds of buildings are there?
- What makes that part of your community special?

2 Label each part of your community.

3 On each sheet write words or sentences that describe the different parts of your community.

4 Use oak tag to make a cover.

5 Staple or sew your book together.

I know all my neighbors. We live on Green Street.

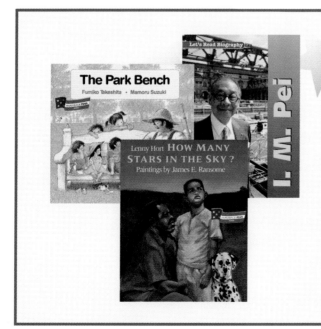

Read On Your Own

Let's Read Biography: I.M. Pei

The Park Bench
by Fumiko Takeshita

How Many Stars in the Sky?
by Lenny Hort

Our Place on Earth

My words are tied in one
With the great mountains.
With the great rocks,
With the great trees,
In one with my body
And my heart.

Yokuts prayer translated by A.L. Kroeber

Key Words

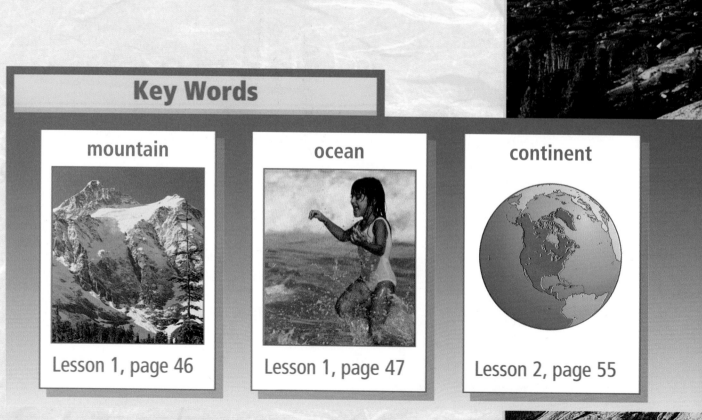

mountain

Lesson 1, page 46

ocean

Lesson 1, page 47

continent

Lesson 2, page 55

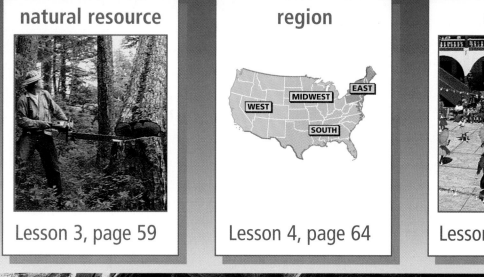

natural resource

Lesson 3, page 59

region

WEST
MIDWEST
EAST
SOUTH

Lesson 4, page 64

culture

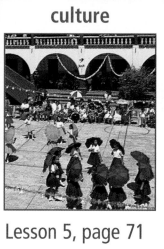

Lesson 5, page 71

43

Land and Water

Main Idea The earth has landforms and bodies of water.

Key Words

plain
mountain
valley
island
ocean
lake
river

Think about the land and water in your community. Do you have to walk up and down hills? Is there a body of water for swimming or boating? As you read, think about how the people in your community use the land and water.

Plain

Different kinds of land are called landforms. A
plain is flat land. Farmers in plains communities use
the land to grow plants or raise animals. There are
also cities on the plains.

Mountain

Some land rises high above the ground. High, steep, land is called a **mountain**. People in mountain communities can hike, ski, or look at the views. Can you think of ways that people in those communities can travel up and down the mountains?

Valley

The land between mountains or hills is called a **valley**. People often build communities in the low land of a valley. The land there is usually good for growing food.

Island

An **island** is land with water all around it. People can use boats, planes, tunnels, or bridges to get on and off island communities. Some islands are very large. Others are very small.

Ocean

Most of the earth is covered by oceans. An **ocean** is a large body of salt water. People living near the ocean can fish, swim, or sail.

Lake

A **lake** is a body of water with land all around it. Some lakes are small. Others are very large. Rain and melted snow help fill lakes with water.

People can use clean lake water for drinking. Some lakes are good for fishing.

River

A **river** is a long, moving body of fresh water. Rivers flow downhill into oceans, lakes, or other rivers. Clean rivers can have water for drinking or for farming. People fish in rivers, too.

Which landforms and bodies of water can you find in your community?

What Did You Learn?

1 **Key Words:** Write these words in sentences to show their meaning: **plain, mountain, island**.

2 Name one difference between a lake and a river.

3 Write about or draw a picture of the land and water in your community.

Let's Explore
Map Skills

Reading a Landform Map

All maps use symbols to stand for real things.
Landform maps use symbols to show water and land.
A symbol can be a color, a shape, or a picture.
Blue usually stands for water. This landform map uses
colors and shapes to show different kinds of land.

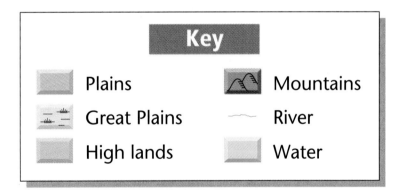

Key

	Plains		Mountains
	Great Plains		River
	High lands		Water

1 **Here's How**

Look at the map key above.

- What does the color yellow stand for on the map?

- What does the color green stand for on the map?

- Compare the symbols for rivers and for mountains. How are they different?

50

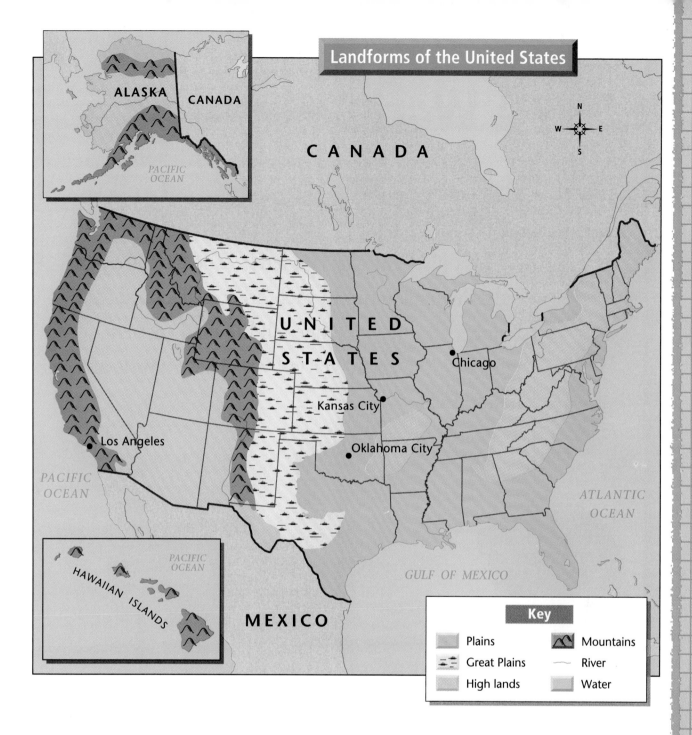

Landforms of the United States

ALASKA CANADA

PACIFIC OCEAN

CANADA

N
W E
S

UNITED STATES

Chicago

Kansas City

Los Angeles

Oklahoma City

PACIFIC OCEAN

ATLANTIC OCEAN

HAWAIIAN ISLANDS

PACIFIC OCEAN

GULF OF MEXICO

MEXICO

Key

Plains

Great Plains

High lands

Mountains

River

Water

❷ Use the Skill

1. Which city on the map is in the mountains?

2. Which landform surrounds Oklahoma City?

3. What do you call the body of water near Chicago?

A World of Places

Main Idea We can describe the earth by its continents, countries, and states.

Lisa just sent Maria a letter. The girls are pen pals. Pen pals write to each other. The words and numbers on the envelope tell the mail carrier where on the earth Maria lives. These words are her address.

Dear Maria,
    There is a great canoe museum in my community. It is a fun place to visit. I saw this kind of canoe there. ... cture of a ... e back

Lisa Ross
95 Clark Road
Peterborough, Ontario
CANADA
K9J4V7

Maria Diaz
523 Seaview Road
Miami Beach, Florida
33139
U.S.A.

52

PACIFIC
OCEAN

UNITED STATES OF AMERICA

ATLANTIC
OCEAN

FLORIDA

GULF
OF
MEXICO

Lisa Ross
95 Clark Road
Peterborough, Ontario
CANADA
K9J 4V7

Maria Diaz
123 Seaview Road
Miami Beach, Florida
33139
U.S.A.

Countries and Nations

The last line in Maria's address says
U.S.A. These letters stand for the United
States of America. That is the name of
our country. A **country** is a land where people
share the same laws and have the same leaders.

Another word for country is **nation**. People live
in many different nations all over the world.

53

States

Maria lives in the state of Florida. A **state** is a smaller place in our country. The United States has 50 states. Look at the map of the United States on pages 226–227. Find Florida and the state where you live.

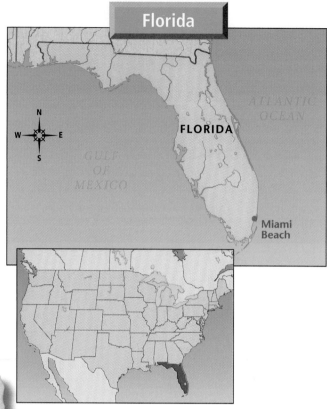

Miami Beach

Cities

The name of Maria's city is Miami Beach. States have cities and towns. Miami Beach is a city on the coast of Florida. A coast is the land next to the ocean. People who live in cities on the coast can fish, swim, or watch many kinds of boats come and go.

Continents

The United States is on the **continent** of North America. A continent is a very large piece of land. There are seven continents on the earth. They are North America, South America, Europe, Africa, Asia, Australia, and Antarctica.

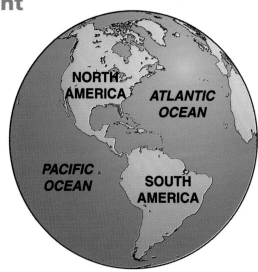

Two other large countries in North America are Mexico and Canada. Lisa lives in Canada. Lisa and Maria live in different countries on the same continent.

What Did You Learn?

1 **Key Words:** Write the name of the **continent**, **country**, and **state** where you live.

2 Describe a coast.

3 Use the map on pages 224–225 to draw the outline of North America on a sheet of paper.

Let's Look
Visual Skills

Reading a Diagram

A diagram is a kind of picture. It can show the parts of something or how it might work. The title tells what the diagram is about. Labels name the parts of the diagram. A straight line connects each part to its label. Maria sent a letter to her pen pal. What does the diagram on the next page show?

❶ Here's How

Look at the diagram of the envelope.

- What is the title of the diagram?

- Find the labels for the two addresses. Who sent the letter? Who received the letter? In what country does Maria's pen pal live?

- What information is on the second line of each address?

Addressing an Envelope

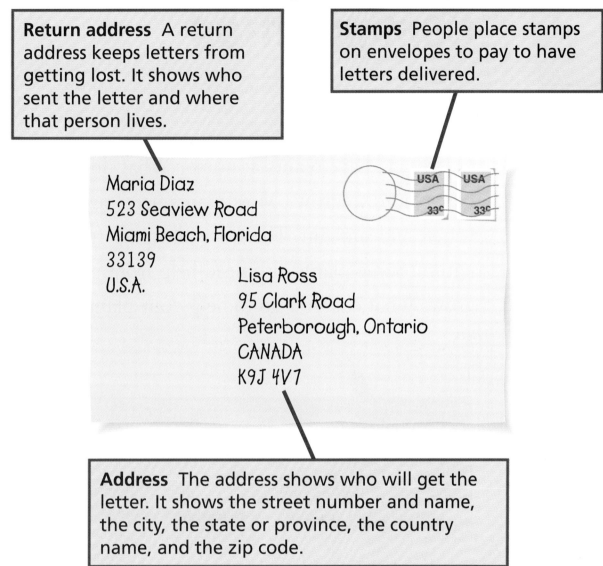

Return address A return address keeps letters from getting lost. It shows who sent the letter and where that person lives.

Stamps People place stamps on envelopes to pay to have letters delivered.

Maria Diaz
523 Seaview Road
Miami Beach, Florida
33139
U.S.A.

Lisa Ross
95 Clark Road
Peterborough, Ontario
CANADA
K9J 4V7

USA USA
33¢ 33¢

Address The address shows who will get the letter. It shows the street number and name, the city, the state or province, the country name, and the zip code.

Use the Skill

1. On what street does Lisa live?

2. When Lisa writes back to Maria, what does she need to write on the first line of the address?

3. Where will Lisa put her own address when she answers Maria's letter?

Resources for Communities

Main Idea People use many resources to grow and make things.

Do you have plants at home? What do your plants need to grow? Most plants need air, soil, water, and sunlight. These are all things from nature. Some plants also need help from people to grow. What can you do to help your plants?

Natural Resources

Just like plants, people need things from nature, too. A **natural resource** is something from nature that people use. Air and soil are natural resources. Trees, rocks, and plants are also natural resources.

drinking

Clean water is an important natural resource. Is your community near a lake or a river? Do people use the lake for drinking water? Everyone needs water for drinking and for washing. Water can be used in other ways too. Look at the photographs to see how people use water.

fighting fires

catching fish

The United States has many natural resources. Some parts of the country have rich soil. It is good for growing plants. We can make bread, cereal, and other foods from plants like wheat. These foods help feed the country's people. The United States also sells its extra wheat to other countries.

growing wheat

Forests grow in some parts of the United States. People use trees to make many things. The chart below shows some things people make from trees.

Made from Trees

cutting down old trees

Trees take a very long time to grow. So tree farmers plant new trees when they cut others down. They do this so more trees will grow.

Planting trees is one way to keep from using up natural resources. What do you think would happen if we didn't use our natural resources wisely? Taking care of natural resources is everyone's job. What can you do to help?

planting new trees

What Did You Learn?

1 **Key Word:** Name two **natural resources**.

2 What are two things people can make from trees?

3 Write about or draw a picture of a natural resource in your community. Tell how people can take care of it.

How Do People Change the Land?

Most landforms and bodies of water are natural. Natural means coming from nature and not made by people.

People can change the land around them by using natural resources. Farmers clear away trees to grow food. People change natural features when they add things to the land such as bridges, homes, and roads.

Science Connection

A dam is a wall built across a river. A dam forms a lake and controls the flow of the lake's water. When water moves through a dam, it has energy. This energy can be turned into electricity. What are some things at home that use electricity?

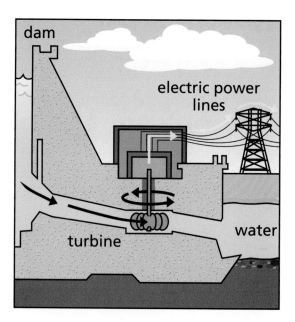

Waterpower makes electricity.

62

People built this bridge to cross the Connecticut River.

Think About It!

1 Look at the photo. List the natural things you see. List the things made by people.

2 Draw a picture that shows how people have changed the land in your community.

LESSON 4

Regions of the U.S.A.

Main Idea Each region of the United States has its own special features.

Key Words

region
crop

If you take a trip around the store, you will see many things that come from other areas of the United States.

When an area of land has features that are the same, it is called a **region**. The features that make up a region might be natural resources, landforms, or weather. Let's look at four regions of the United States. What is special about each one?

64

Regions of the United States

Seattle

MIDWEST

Chicago

Indianapolis

WEST

EAST

New York City

PACIFIC OCEAN

Los Angeles

Phoenix

SOUTH

Atlanta

ATLANTIC OCEAN

New Orleans

Wood is made into paper at a mill.

West

Look at the map above. Find the West. It is near the Pacific Ocean. This region has many mountains, deserts, and forests. Trees are an important natural resource here.

Midwest

The Midwest is another region. The soil in the Midwest is rich, so the region has many large farms. Farmers grow crops such as corn, wheat, and soybeans. A **crop** is a plant a farmer grows and gathers.

A farmer cuts corn.

65

People in the East fish on the Atlantic Ocean.

East

The East is near the Atlantic Ocean. Its coast has good, deep harbors. A harbor is a place where ships can stop safely. Shipping and fishing are important in the East.

South

People in the South grow many crops in rich soil. Cities in the South have become important business centers. Many companies move from other regions to the South. Some families move to this region because they like warm weather.

Peanuts grow on farms in the South.

When you return home from your trip to the store, you will see many things in your bag. They might remind you of the four regions of our country. Look at the picture below to see where each item came from. Don't forget the paper bag!

What Did You Learn?

1 **Key Words:** Use **region** in a sentence to show its meaning.

2 What is one difference between the East and the Midwest?

3 Write or tell about something you might see or do in each region of the United States.

Using a Dictionary

Here is a riddle for you: What book has words, but no story? The answer is a dictionary. A dictionary is a book that tells what words mean and how to say and spell them. Let's find the word *country* on this dictionary page.

count ◇ cowb

count
To **count** means to
on her desk. There

country
1. A **country** is
people in on
many citi

❶ Here's How

- The words in a dictionary are in ABC order. To find *country,* you look in the section with the words that begin with C. Which letter comes before C in the alphabet? Which letter follows C?

- After you find the C section you need to find the right page. The guide words at the top of each page help. The guide words show the first and last words on a page.

- What is the first word on this page?

count
To **count** means to add. Kate **counted** the pencils on her desk. There were five pencils.

country
1. A **country** is a place where people live. All the people in one **country** share the same laws. There are many cities and towns in a **country**. There are many **countries** in the world. 2. The **country** is an area away from a city. There are forests, fields, and farms in the **country**. —**countries**

cousin
Your **cousin** is the child of your aunt or uncle. Ted has lots of **cousins**.

cover
1. To **cover** means to put something on top of something else. Wendy **covered** herself with thick blankets to keep warm. 2. A **cover** goes on the top or outside of something. Books have **covers**. Pots and pans also have **covers**.

cover

cow
A **cow** is a large animal that lives on a farm. **Cows** give milk.

cowboy
A **cowboy** is a man who takes care of cattle. **Cowboys** work on big farms. They often ride horses.

cow

66

cowgirl
A **cowgirl** is a woman who takes care of cattle. **Cowgirls** work on big farms. They often ride horses.

crack
A **crack** is a small broken place. It looks like a crooked line. The mirror had **cracks** in it.

cowboy

crash
1. To **crash** means to hit something and break with a lot of noise. We saw two cars **crash** into each other. 2. A **crash** is a loud noise. We heard a **crash** in the next room.

crawl
To **crawl** is to move on your hands and knees. Babies **crawl** until they learn to walk.

crayon
A **crayon** is a piece of colored wax. It is used to draw and write with. **Crayons** come in many colors.

❷ Use the Skill

1. What does the word *country* mean?

2. Why does *country* come before *crayon*?

3. Suppose you want to find the word *fun* in the dictionary. Which pair of guide words would help you? Why?

foot/for   **fuel/fur**

69

North American Neighbors

Main Idea Canada and Mexico are our neighbors in North America.

People living in communities usually have neighbors. Nations have neighbors, too. The United States has two next-door neighbors. Canada is our neighbor to the north and Mexico is to the south. The three countries are friends. Countries that are friendly get along. People can go back and forth between them. Find these countries on the map.

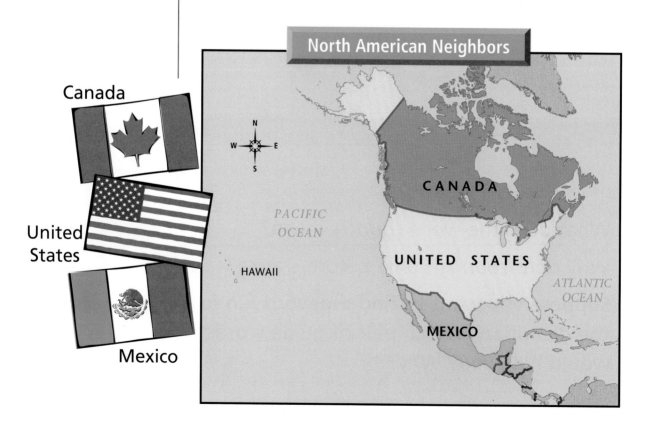

North American Neighbors

Canada

United States

Mexico

70

Every country has its own culture. **Culture** is the way of life shared by a group of people. You can see it in how people work, play, and even build their homes. People of the same culture share art, music, folktales, and past events. Foods can be a part of culture, too.

Calgary Stampede, Canada

a graduation, Mexico

People of the same culture can share beliefs. **Beliefs** are ideas that people think are true. You and your family may have the same beliefs as other people who go to your church, temple, or mosque.

The people of Canada, Mexico, and the United States come from different cultures. Let's learn about our neighbors, Canada and Mexico.

Canada

Canada is the second largest country in the world. Like the United States, Canada's land stretches from the Atlantic coast of North America to the Pacific coast. Its land almost reaches the North Pole. That part of Canada has cold weather all year long.

The parts of Canada near the United States have four seasons. The winters in Canada are cold and long. Many people like winter sports. The summers are warm there.

Hundreds of years ago, the Inuit (IHN-yu-iht) and other Native Americans lived in Canada. They hunted and fished to get their food. Then people from France, Great Britain, and other countries came to Canada. They hunted for animals with fur. They sold the fur to make money.

Those new people brought their languages with them. A **language** is the words that people speak, read, and write. Language is part of every culture. English and French are the main languages used in Canada today.

Mexico

Mexico is our neighbor to the south. The weather there is much warmer than in Canada and most of the United States. Mexico's land is very different from one place to another. Mexico has many mountains. It has beautiful beaches on its coasts. It also has many forests.

The earliest people who lived in Mexico were Native Americans. Two groups were the Maya (MY yuh) and the Aztec. They built cities and dug for silver and gold.

Later, people from Spain came to Mexico. Spain is a country in Europe. The Spanish brought their language and culture with them. Today, people in Mexico speak Spanish.

Today, visitors to Mexico see old Native American cities. They can also see new cities with skyscrapers. Many people in Mexico still live in small towns. In the middle of the town is a plaza. It is a place where people meet friends and neighbors. Would you like to move to Canada or Mexico? How would your life change?

What Did You Learn?

1 **Key Words:** What is **language**? Name three languages that people who live in North America might speak.

2 Name three countries in North America.

3 Compare the land of Mexico and Canada with the land of the United States.

Let's Explore
Map Skills

Using a World Map

The earth is round like a ball. A globe is a model of the earth. A globe shows the true shape of the earth's land and water. On a globe, we can see the world's oceans and continents.

World maps also show all the earth's land and water. Maps are flat. The shapes of the earth's land and water look different on a world map.

You can use a globe to find the directions North and South. The North Pole and South Pole help you tell directions on a globe. On a map, a compass rose shows the letters N, S, E, and W to help find directions.

① Here's How

- Compare the world map with the globe.
- What helps you know directions on a globe and on a map?

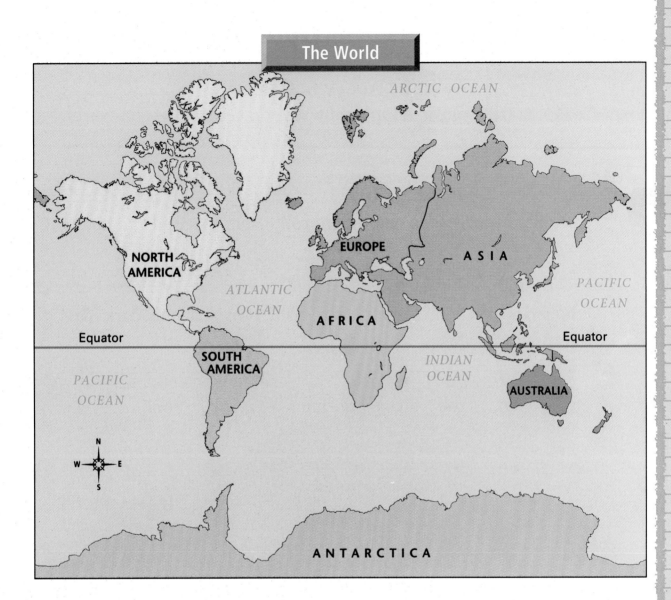

❷ Use the Skills

1. Look at the world map. What are the seven continents?

2. What are the names of the four oceans on the earth?

3. When could you use a world map?

Roll On, Columbia

words by Woody Guthrie
music adapted by Woody Guthrie

Chorus

Roll on,— Co-lum-bia, roll on. Roll on,— Co-lum-bia, roll on. Your pow-er is turn-ing our dark-ness to dawn, So, roll on, Co-lum-bia, roll on!

Green Doug-las firs where the wa-ters cut through.

Down her wild moun-tains and can-yons she flew. Can-a-di-an North-west to the o-ceans so blue,

Roll on, Co-lum-bia, roll on!

Douglas fir—a tall pine tree that grows in the northwestern part of North America

canyon—a deep valley with steep walls

dawn—the time in the morning when the sun rises

mightiest—showing the greatest strength

Other great rivers add power to you,
Yakima, Snake, and the Klickitat, too,
Sandy, Willamette, and the Hood River, too,
Roll on, Columbia, roll on!
Chorus

And on up the river is Grand Coulee Dam,
The mightiest thing ever built by a man,
To run the great factories and water the land, it's
Roll on, Columbia, roll on!
Chorus

Response Activity

Make a list of all the landforms and bodies of water in the song.

Theme 2
Review

Theme 2 Big Ideas

1. Write or say one thing you learned about each of the pictures below.

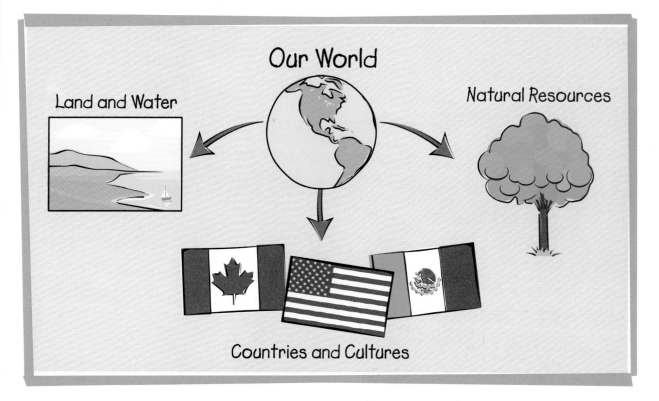

Our World

Land and Water

Natural Resources

Countries and Cultures

Review What You Learned

2. List three things in your classroom that are made from trees.

3. What landform has water all around it?

4. What country in North America is south of the United States?

5. Name one thing that is part of a person's culture.

Key Words

Use the key words below to fill in the sentences.

continent (p. 55)   natural resource (p. 59)
culture (p. 71)   ocean (p. 47)
mountain (p. 46)   region (p. 64)

6. The _____ we live on is North America.

7. A _____ is steep land that rises high above the ground.

8. Soil is a _____ _____.

9. An _____ is a large body of salt water.

10. Each _____ of the United States has its own resources, landforms, and weather.

11. Our _____ includes the way we speak, dress, and the foods we eat.

Write a Letter

12. Write a letter to a friend. Tell your friend about a pretend trip to Mexico. Answer these questions in your letter.

    • In what direction did you travel?

    • What language did people there speak?

    • What interesting things did you see?

Dear Jane,
    I am going to Mexico. I will fly on a plane.

Use the landform map on the right to answer the questions.

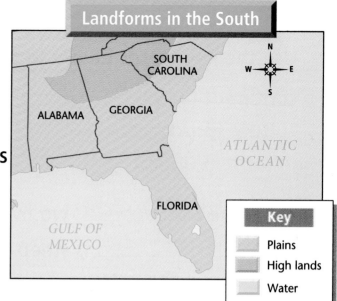

Landforms in the South

SOUTH
CAROLINA

ALABAMA   GEORGIA

ATLANTIC
OCEAN

FLORIDA

GULF OF
MEXICO

Key

Plains
High lands
Water

13. Compare the land of Florida and Georgia. Which state has both plains and high lands?

14. Which states on this map have plains?

15. Look at the map on pages 222–223. Name two continents with coasts on the Atlantic Ocean.

Use the diagram below to answer the questions.

16. Under what does this tunnel go?

17. What brings air into the tunnel?

18. Use a dictionary to find the word *tunnel*. What are the guide words on the page? What does *tunnel* mean?

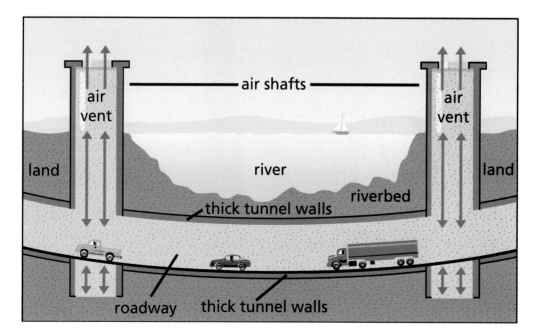

air shafts

air
vent

air
vent

land   river   land

riverbed

thick tunnel walls

roadway   thick tunnel walls

Make a Regional Diorama

1 Choose a region of the United States. Make or draw the landforms and large bodies of water in that region.

2 Paste or place the landforms and bodies of water in the shoe box.

3 Add a natural resource that is found in that region.

4 Write a label telling one way people use that resource.

5 Add other labels to tell about the region.

6 You may want to cover the outside of the box with paper.

Things You'll Need

- construction paper
- scissors
- clay
- crayons or markers
- paste
- a shoe box

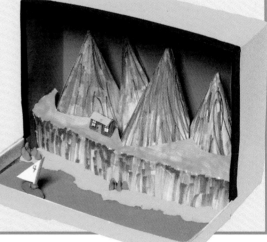

Read On Your Own

It Takes a Village
by Jane Cowen-Fletcher

**Let's Read Biography:
Christa McAuliffe**

People at Work

Minnie spent her money on a frozen lemon-lime.
Now she hasn't any — not a penny, not a dime!
"Better save your money, Minnie, maybe you should try:
There will be another day with other things to buy!"

"Minnie" by Ruth I. Dowell

Key Words

needs	job	goods
Lesson 1, page 87	Lesson 2, page 93	Lesson 2, page 94

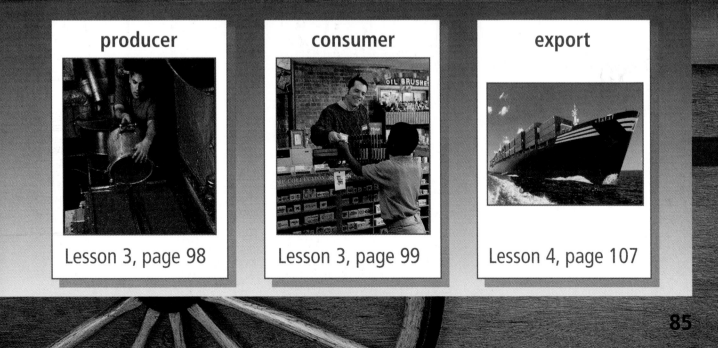

producer	consumer	export
Lesson 3, page 98	Lesson 3, page 99	Lesson 4, page 107

ITALIAN ICE WORLD FAMOUS

Lemon & Watermelon

LESSON 1

People Have Needs

Main Idea People work to make money so that they can pay for what they need.

Key Words

needs
shelter
income

What did you do before you came to school today? You woke up. You got dressed for school. Maybe you ate breakfast.

Everyone in the world needs food to eat, clothes to wear, and a place to live. In our country, all of these things cost money.

86

Meeting Our Needs

Needs are things that people must have to live. All people have needs. You and your family need food, clothing, and a place to live.

Food is very important. Foods like vegetables, fruits, milk, bread, and meat help bodies grow and stay healthy. What is your favorite food?

Clothing is another need. Clothes protect your body from different kinds of weather. On cold days, you wear clothes that will keep you warm. On hot days, you choose clothes that will keep you cool. What clothes do you wear on a rainy day?

A **shelter** is something that protects or covers. Your home is a shelter. Shelters keep out rain, snow, or heat.

In regions where it snows often, people build homes with steep roofs so that snow will fall off. Homes in the South can have flat roofs to protect people from hot sun and pouring rains.

Paying for Needs

How do people get food, clothing, and shelter? Long ago, many people hunted, fished, and grew their own food. Today, people in our country work to earn money to buy the things they need. The money they earn is part of their **income**.

People also use income to pay for things they want. A want is something someone would like to have, but does not have to have.

Most families cannot buy everything they want. They make choices about how to spend their income. Often, people save until they have enough money to pay for the things they want. Many people save their money in a bank. Banks keep money safe.

Mom, We need: milk, bread, and eggs. Can you buy some cookies too? Thanks.

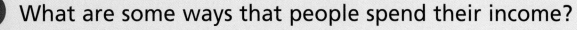

What Did You Learn?

1. **Key Words:** Give an example of a **need**.
2. What are some ways that people spend their income?
3. Write about or draw a picture of a shelter.

★ CITIZENSHIP ★

Making Choices

Making choices can be hard. When you make a choice, you must give up something. In order to make good choices, people need good information.

Toys or Good Deeds?

In Utah some fast-food restaurants give away toys with their meals. The students at Whittier Elementary School worried that the toys were a waste of money.

The students asked 600 children what they did with the meal toys. Most did not keep the toys. The students wrote letters to the restaurants, telling what they had learned.

Instead of spending money for toys, the class asked the restaurants to give the money to community groups that did good deeds. The students voted for four groups that did good things for other people. They made place mats for the restaurants. The place mats show the four groups that get money from the restaurants.

Changes for Our School
1. More playground equipment.
2. Better lunches.
3. More computers.

Good citizens make choices to help their community.

You Take Action

1. List some things that your class would like to do to help your school.
2. Ask other classes to choose their favorite idea from your list. Tally the results. List the three ideas that got the most tallies. Then vote for the idea you like best.
3. Write a letter to the principal that tells about your choice.

★ Tips for Making Choices ★

- Start with many ideas.
- Discuss the ideas before you vote for one.

LESSON 2

Jobs in Our Community

Main Idea People in a community have many different jobs.

Key Words
job
goods
factory
service

It takes many people to do all the work in a community. David took pictures of the workers you see on these two pages.

92

Jobs

A **job** is the work that someone does to earn an income. Occupation (awk u PAY shun) is another word for job. Writing books, cutting hair, teaching, and farming are all jobs. Think of some jobs that people do in your community.

For most jobs, people need to have special skills. They go to school to learn the skills they need for their jobs. What would you like to do someday? How can you prepare for the job you want in the future? David wants to be a photographer.

Goods

The things that people make or grow to sell are called **goods**. Food is one kind of good. Some people make goods at home or in small shops. Others grow food for people to eat.

Trucks, video games, and shoes are all goods. A **factory** is a building where people work together to make goods. Factory workers use machines to do some of their work.

Services

Many workers have jobs that help other people. These workers provide a **service**. Service workers do not make or grow goods that you can buy and take home in a bag.

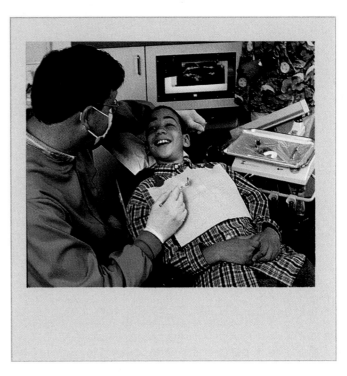

Service workers make our lives easier. They do things we cannot always do for ourselves. For example, a dentist helps you take care of your teeth. A bus driver takes you from place to place. In our country, many people work at jobs that provide services.

What Did You Learn?

1. **Key Words:** Write an example of each of the following: **job, goods, service**.

2. Does a police officer make goods or provide a service?

3. Write about or draw a picture of a job you would like to have when you grow up.

Trade

Have you ever traded a part of your lunch or baseball cards with friends? When people want or need something, they sometimes can trade to get it. They give up one thing to get another in return. The things people use to trade have changed over time.

Then

Long ago in Greece, when people needed food, clothing, or other goods, they traded things such as salt and fish. This kind of trade is called barter.

Now → Today, most people use money to buy goods and services. They also use checks and credit cards to buy things. What do you use to buy the things you want?

Think About It!

1 What do most people use today to pay for goods and services?

2 Think About the Future: Write about or draw three ways you think people will pay for things in the future. Share your ideas with a friend.

97

Making Goods for Everyone

Main Idea Many people work together to make and sell products.

Products are goods that are made. Long ago, people made products such as clothes, toys, and other things by hand. Today, most products are made by machines in a factory. When factory workers make something, they **manufacture** it.

When you make or grow a product, you are a **producer**. Workers who provide a service are producers, too.

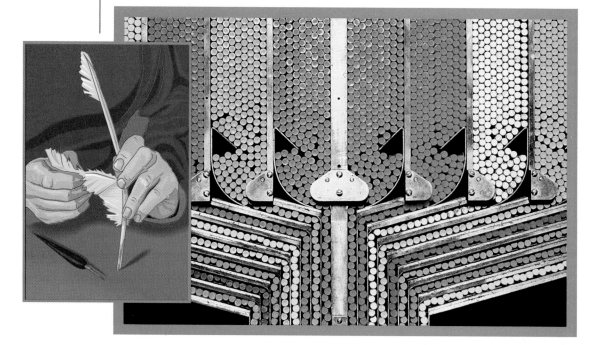

Long ago, pens had to be made by hand, but today people can use machines to make crayons.

Have you ever bought a box of crayons? Have you ever gotten your hair cut? When you do these things, you are a consumer. A **consumer** is someone who buys or uses goods or services. Everyone in a community is a consumer of something. Can you think of a way that you were a consumer today?

People can be both producers and consumers. When people make things or provide services, we call them producers. When they use their money to buy goods and services, they are consumers.

Producing Crayons

One manufactured product you use every day is crayons. Most crayons are made in factories. One crayon factory in the United States makes more than two billion crayons a year. In one day the factory makes enough crayons to fill a giant statue taller than the Statue of Liberty.

Crayons are made of wax. Wax is a product of oil, a natural resource that comes from the ground.

A tanker train brings melted wax to the factory. Heated train cars keep the wax melted. The heated wax is stored in very large tanks until it is needed.

In the factory, workers begin making crayons. They pump the wax into large heated pots or kettles. Then different colors are added to each kettle. When the colored wax is ready, it is poured into a mold. The mold has thousands of holes shaped like crayons.

Cold water cools the mold to harden the wax. Soon after this, thousands of crayons come out of the molds!

Now the crayons need labels that tell the colors and the name of the company. A machine wraps the label around each crayon.

Finally, machines sort the new crayons and pack them in boxes.

Buying Crayons

The crayons are sent to stores all over the world. Consumers, like you, can now buy new crayons.

How does the crayon company decide what price to charge for crayons? **Price** is the amount of money consumers pay for goods or services.

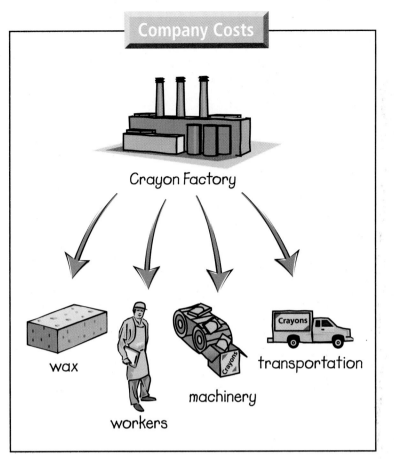

Company Costs

Crayon Factory

wax

workers

machinery

transportation

Crayons

To set a price, the company must know what it costs to make the crayons. This chart shows some costs at a crayon factory.

The company charges more for the crayons than it costs to make them. The difference between the price of the crayons and the costs of making them is the company's profit. Companies try to set the price of products to make a profit.

What Did You Learn?

1 **Key Words:** Use each of these words in a sentence: **manufacture, producer, consumer**.

2 What does a company need to know to set a price for a product?

3 Use crayons to draw a picture that shows how crayons are made.

Reading a Flow Chart

We all know that milk comes from cows. Do you know how milk gets from the cow to a store? This flow chart shows you. A **flow chart** shows the steps to make or do something. The title tells about the flow chart. The arrows show the way to follow the steps.

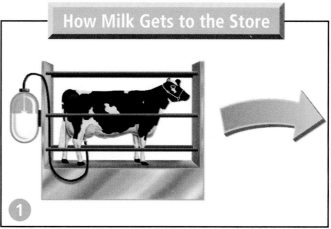

How Milk Gets to the Store

① Here's How

Look at this part of a flow chart.

- What is the title?
- Which step does this part of the flow chart show?
- What does the arrow mean?

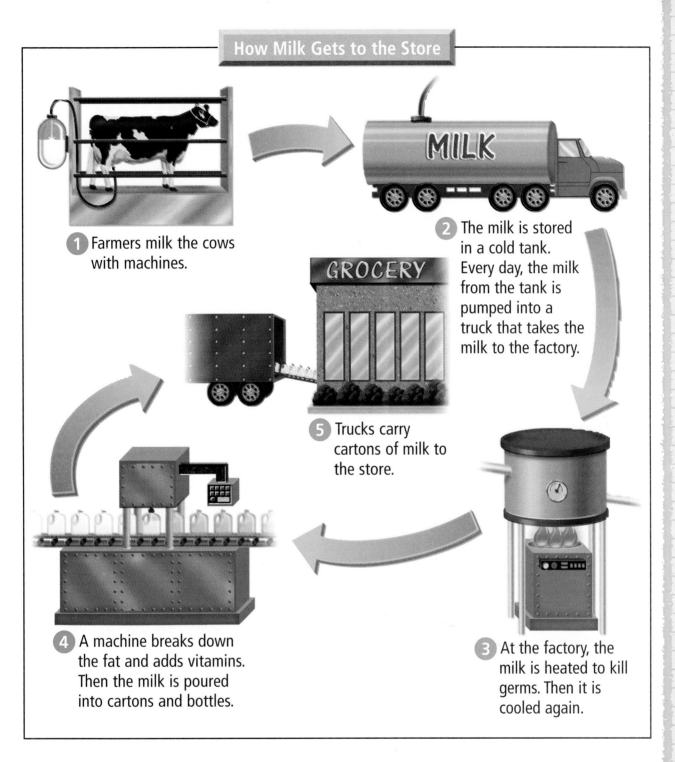

How Milk Gets to the Store

1. Farmers milk the cows with machines.

2. The milk is stored in a cold tank. Every day, the milk from the tank is pumped into a truck that takes the milk to the factory.

3. At the factory, the milk is heated to kill germs. Then it is cooled again.

4. A machine breaks down the fat and adds vitamins. Then the milk is poured into cartons and bottles.

5. Trucks carry cartons of milk to the store.

2 **Use the Skill**

1. What is the fourth step in this flow chart?

2. What is done to kill germs?

3. How does the milk get from the factory to the store?

Goods on the Move

Main Idea Countries around the world trade goods and services.

It is hard for every country in the world to produce all the things its people want. So countries trade goods and services, just as people do.

You may have products at home that come from another country. Check the labels on clothes and toys to find out where they were made. All countries do not make the same products or grow the same foods. Countries sell some of their goods and services. Then they have the money to buy the things they cannot make.

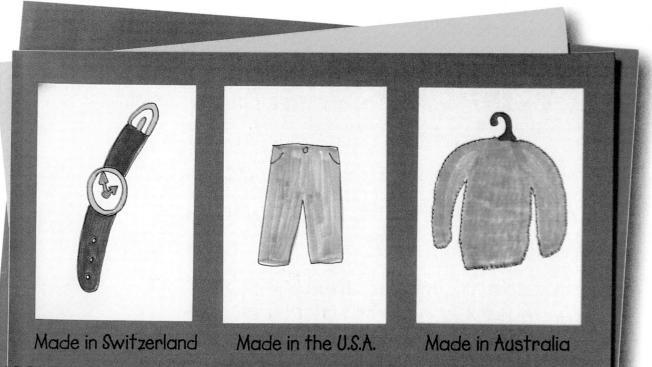

Made in Switzerland   Made in the U.S.A.   Made in Australia

106

Exporting Goods

Factories in the United States make many kinds of goods, like cars and tractors. Companies in the United States export cars and tractors to other nations. To **export** means to sell and send goods to other countries. Farmers in the United States grow food such as wheat and soybeans. The United States exports its extra food to other countries, too. We export food to nations such as Brazil, Saudi Arabia, and Japan. Can you find these nations on the map on page 108?

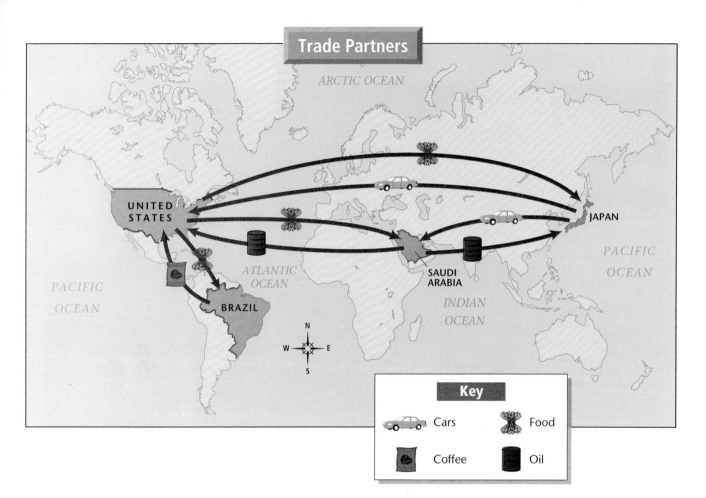

Key

Cars   Food

Coffee   Oil

Importing Goods

To **import** means to buy things from other countries. For example, Saudi Arabia, a country in the Middle East, produces more oil than it can use. The United States needs more oil than it has. Companies in the United States import oil from Saudi Arabia to make gasoline, crayons, and other goods. Large ships called tankers bring the oil across the Indian and Atlantic oceans to the United States.

Moving Goods to Market

Companies need different kinds of transportation to move goods from place to place. Trucks and trains carry goods over land. Ships carry products across oceans. Cargo planes fly goods over land and sea. Trucks, trains, ships, and planes carry freight, or goods, to the places where the goods can be sold.

What Did You Learn?

1 **Key Words:** Tell the differences between **import** and **export**.

2 Name four ways goods are moved from place to place.

3 Write about or draw something you use that comes from another country.

Using a Map Scale

Think about drawing a picture of a building. Is your picture the same size as the real thing? A map is a kind of drawing, too. It shows a smaller picture of a place. You can use maps to find out how far one place is from another. When you do this, you find distance.

To figure out distance on a map, you use the map scale. A scale tells how much smaller the map is than the real place. On a scale, one inch on a map might stand for one mile of land. Scales can change from map to map.

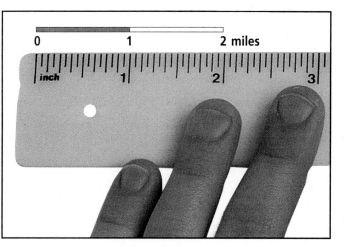

❶ Here's How

Look at the map scale.

- What does the scale show?

- What tool can you use to measure distance on a map?

- What distance does one inch stand for on this map?

110

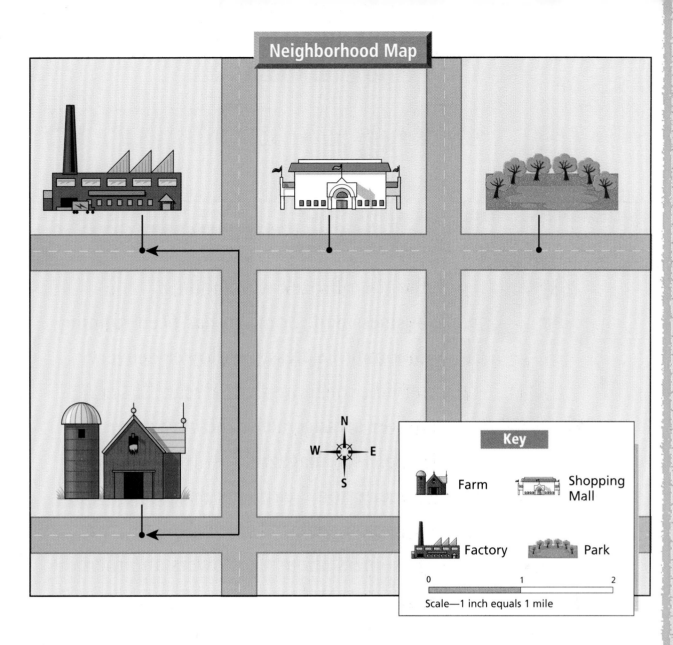

Neighborhood Map

2 Use the Skill

1. How many inches is it on the map from the shopping mall to the factory?

2. How many miles is it from the real shopping mall to the factory? Use the scale to find out.

3. By road, how many miles is it from the farm to the factory?

Sweet Jobs:
KIDS IN BUSINESS

Nice Arrangement

Brandon Brozek is a budding businessman. Brandon has been running Bloomin' Express, his flower delivery service, for more than a year. "I sell flower arrangements the way other people sell magazines — by subscription," explains Brandon, 11, of Miami, Florida. "I like telling my customers about the flowers and then delivering them."

Brandon claims that Bloomin' Express flowers last longer than arrangements from supermarkets. "They're fresher," he explains.

Each week Brandon finds out what his nine subscribers want, phones in the orders to the supplier, and — with his father's help — makes deliveries.

Sometimes Brandon's mother lends a hand, too. "My mom is great about helping me figure taxes and keep records — things I haven't learned to do yet," Brandon says.

Making Dough With Cookies

Whether it's making cookies or making change, Tardkeith McBride and Maurice Cobb learn how to handle dough at Champ Cookies & Things in Washington, D.C. Tardkeith, 14, on the left, and Maurice, 15, are among more than 65 young people who operate the factory.

Ali Khan, a former teacher and school guidance counselor, started Champ Cookies four years ago with three friends. Their idea was to help keep youngsters out of the crime and drug world. "We teach them how a business runs and encourage them to take pride in their work," Khan says.

Working for a few hours after school each day, the students learn every step of the business.

In Business With Birds

Nikky Hoyne will never get caught with all her eggs in one basket. They wouldn't fit. Nikky, 9, of Hinsdale, Illinois, sells as many as seven dozen eggs a day. When she began keeping chickens as pets four years ago, she gave the eggs away. Now Nikky has about 25 customers who buy them on a regular basis. "People like my eggs because they are so good and so fresh," she says. Nikky spends several hours a day caring for chicks and feeding, cleaning, and playing with her hens. For Nikky it's a labor of love. "My chickens are my friends," she explains.

Response Activity

Write about a business you would like to run. Tell how your business would provide a service or goods to others.

Theme 3 Big Ideas

1. Write a sentence telling about the pictures and words below.

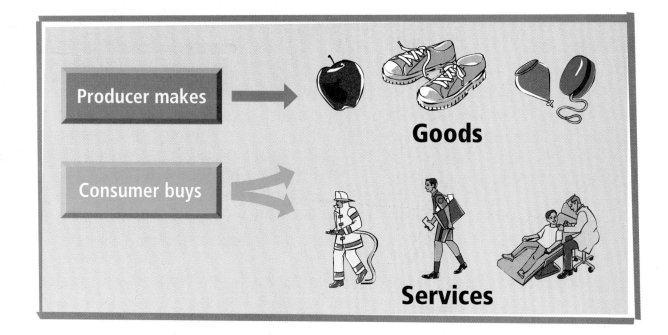

Producer makes → Goods

Consumer buys → Services

Review What You Learned

2. What are needs and wants?

3. Where can people keep the money that they earn?

4. Does a doctor provide a good or a service?

5. What are three ways that goods are carried from one country to another?

Key Words

Use the key words below to fill in the sentences.

consumer (p. 99)   job (p. 93)
export (p. 107)   needs (p. 87)
goods (p. 94)   producer (p. 98)

6. The work a person does to earn a living is called a _____.

7. Computers and televisions are _____ that stores sell.

8. Shelter, clothes, and food are _____.

9. A factory worker who helps make clothes is a _____.

10. A _____ is a person who buys goods and services.

11. Countries _____ products they make to other nations.

Write an Ad for a Job

12. Your town has asked you to write a "Help Wanted" ad. They are looking for a lifeguard to work at the town pool this summer. Create an ad for the job that answers these questions:

   • What skills and training must a lifeguard have?

   • What does a lifeguard do?

   • How does this service help people?

Help Wanted: Lifeguard

Use the map on the right to answer the questions.

Community Map

13. How many miles is it from the school to the post office?

14. Is it shorter to go from the school to the post office or from the school to the park?

15. How far is it from the park to the library?

Key

School   Post Office

Library   Park

0   1   2

Scale—1 inch equals 1 mile

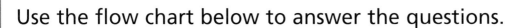

Use the flow chart below to answer the questions.

16. What is the chart about?

17. What happens in step 1?

18. Are the wheels added before or after the axles?

How to Make a Delivery Truck

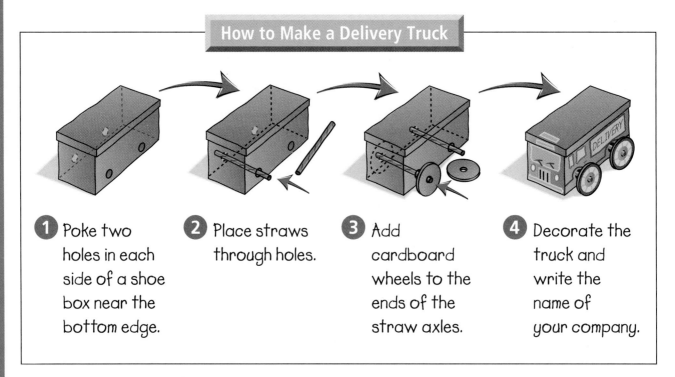

1 Poke two holes in each side of a shoe box near the bottom edge.

2 Place straws through holes.

3 Add cardboard wheels to the ends of the straw axles.

4 Decorate the truck and write the name of your company.

Make a Job Concentration Game

1 Brainstorm with your group. Write a list of jobs. Make sure some jobs produce goods and some provide services.

Things You'll Need
- index cards
- crayons or markers

2 Write each job's name on a card. Put the cards in a big box. Everyone can reach in and pick one card.

3 Read the name on the card. On another card, write and draw what that worker does.

4 Collect all the cards. Mix them up.

5 Place all the cards on a table or floor, face down. Take turns making matches.

firefighter

Read On Your Own

Let's Read Biography
Eleanor Roosevelt

Something from Nothing
by Phoebe Gilman

Abuela's Weave
by Omar S. Castañeda

Our Nation's Story

Lo que yo más amo, es la Libertad; nunca, a un pajarito, ni a nadie se la he de quitar.	What I love the most is freedom; not from a bird, nor from anyone, shall I ever take it away, ever.
"La libertad" by A.L. Jáurengui	"Liberty" Translated by Angela de Hoyos

Key Words

history

Lesson 1, page 122

explorer

Lesson 2, page 126

colonist

Lesson 2, page 130

vote

Lesson 3, page 139

pioneer

Lesson 4, page 143

immigrant

Lesson 5, page 150

The First Americans

Main Idea Long ago, many groups of Native Americans built communities all over the Americas.

Key Words

history
honor

You may have heard people in your family tell stories about long ago. These stories are your family history. **History** is the story of the past and the people who came before us.

The oldest stories of North America come from Native Americans. Older people pass down stories to younger people. This is one way we know about the people who came before us.

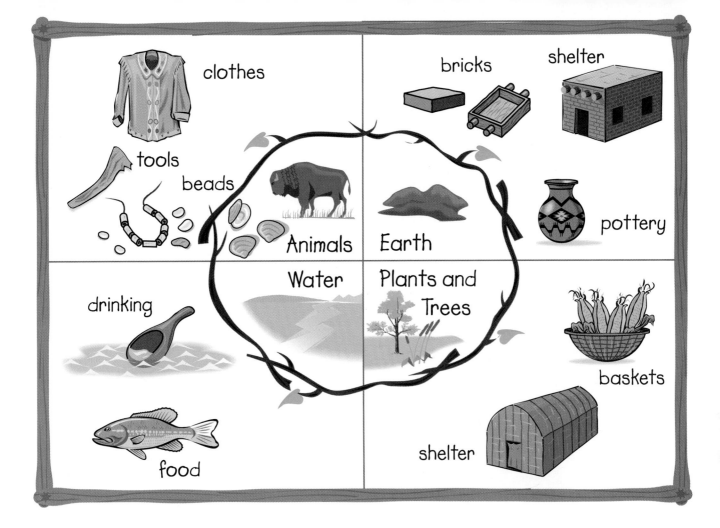

clothes

bricks

shelter

tools

beads

Animals

Earth

pottery

drinking

Water

Plants and Trees

baskets

food

shelter

Native Americans lived in all parts of North America. They were here long before people from other countries came. Some groups made their homes in forests. Others lived on the plains, in the mountains, or in the desert. Every group used natural resources. They used wood, animal skins, or clay to build homes. The land and water gave them food, too.

Most Native Americans honor the land and nature. **Honor** means to show respect for someone or something. People hold ceremonies to mark important events such as a wedding or the birth of a baby. A ceremony is an act that honors people or events.

Apache fiddle

123

The Muscogee

Muscogee (muh skoh GEE) people lived on land that is now part of the states of Alabama, Georgia, and Florida. They built communities along the creeks and rivers in the region. Men hunted in nearby forests. Women gathered nuts, onions, and fruit. Families worked together to grow corn, beans, squash, and pumpkins.

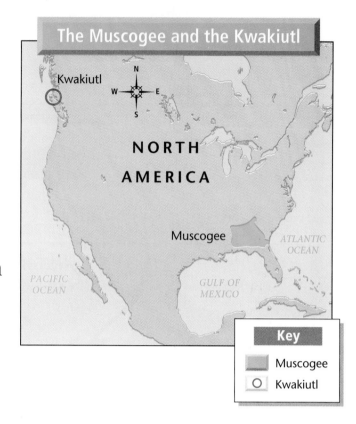

The Muscogee and the Kwakiutl

NORTH AMERICA

Kwakiutl

Muscogee

PACIFIC OCEAN

GULF OF MEXICO

ATLANTIC OCEAN

Key
Muscogee
O Kwakiutl

Every summer the Muscogee held the Green Corn ceremony to give thanks for the food they had grown and gathered. Before the ceremony people cleaned and fixed up their homes. They made peace with neighbors. They performed dances and ate a big meal. Many Muscogee still hold the Green Corn ceremony.

This Muscogee woman is making sofkee, a drink made from corn.

124

The Kwakiutl

Kwakiutl (Kwah kee OO duhl) people live on the west coast of North America. They built communities along the Pacific Ocean where there were forests and mountains. The Kwakiutl fished in the ocean and dug clams for food.

The Kwakiutl used cedar trees for many things. They built homes with cedar boards. They also made boxes, totem poles, clothes, and hats with wood from cedar trees. Kwakiutl artists carved large canoes for fishing and trading. The Kwakiutl today know these skills from the people who lived before them.

What Did You Learn?

1. **Key Word:** What does **history** mean?

2. Long ago, how did the Muscogee and the Kwakiutl use the land and water around them?

3. Draw a picture of a ceremony you have seen or were part of. Tell why it was important.

Explorers and Settlers

Main Idea People from Europe came to America for different reasons.

Key Words
explorer
settler
colony
colonist

Hundreds of years ago, most people in Europe, Asia, and Africa did not know about the continents of North and South America. Sailors from Europe went a long way around Africa to trade for goods in Asia.

Leaders in Europe sent explorers to find a faster way to get to Asia. An **explorer** is a person who travels to a new place to learn new things.

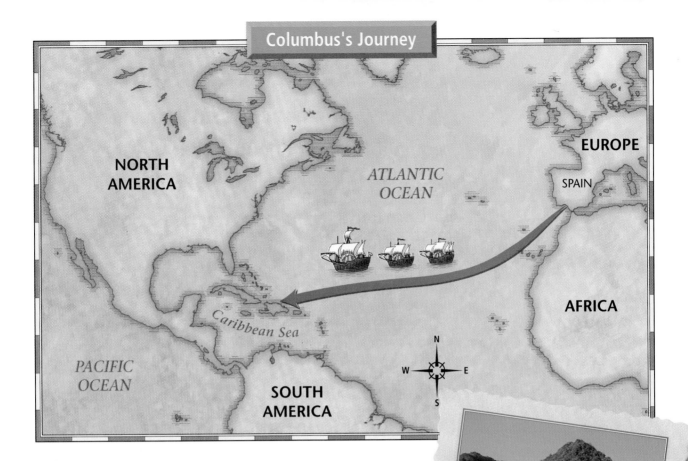

NORTH
AMERICA

ATLANTIC
OCEAN

EUROPE

SPAIN

Caribbean Sea

AFRICA

PACIFIC
OCEAN

SOUTH
AMERICA

N
W E
S

A Caribbean Island

Christopher Columbus

One explorer was Christopher
Columbus. He sailed west from Spain to
look for a new way to Asia. About 90
men and boys sailed with him across
the Atlantic Ocean. He had three
ships: the *Niña*, the *Pinta*, and the
Santa María.

On October 12, 1492, Columbus
landed on an island in the Caribbean Sea. He did not
know he was in the Americas. Look at the map to see
where Columbus landed. Native Americans were already
living on the island. Still Columbus said that all the land
and gold he found there belonged to Spain.

127

Settlers Come to America

After Columbus returned to Spain, many people found out about his trip. More explorers followed. They wanted to find riches and to own land in the Americas. Some wanted to settle there.

A **settler** is a person who moves to a new place to make a home. Some of the first settlers were soldiers. Other people came to spread their beliefs about God. Then families came from Europe to build houses and towns.

A Spanish carving made more than 300 years ago

St. Augustine

The king and queen of Spain wanted to own the land we call Florida. They sent Pedro Menéndez de Avilés (PEY droh mehn EHN dehz deh ah vee LEHZ) with soldiers to take this land for Spain. The French also wanted land in Florida. Spanish soldiers built a town called St. Augustine in 1565. They fought with French soldiers to keep their town.

St. Augustine is the oldest Spanish settlement in the United States. You can visit the fort and see where soldiers lived long ago.

St. Augustine, Florida

129

Plymouth

The Pilgrims

In 1620, a group of settlers sailed to North America from England. This group, called the Pilgrims, started a colony. A **colony** is a place that is ruled by another country. A person who lives in a colony is called a **colonist**.

The Pilgrims left England because they were not free to live and pray the way they wanted. They sailed on a ship called the *Mayflower*. The Pilgrims called the place where they settled Plymouth.

Plymouth, Massachusetts

The Pilgrims worked hard to build their colony. They tried to get ready for the long winter in their new home. Many colonists, however, grew sick in the first winter and died.

Then, a Native American named Squanto taught the Pilgrims how to plant corn. They had not grown corn in England. He also showed them how to catch fish and where to hunt. Without Squanto's help, the Plymouth colony might not have lasted.

What Did You Learn?

1 **Key Words:** Write the meaning of the words **explorer** and **settler**.

2 Why did Columbus sail from Spain?

3 Write or draw a picture describing life for a Pilgrim in Plymouth.

Shelter

Shelter protects you from rain or snow. It keeps out the hot sun. That is true today. It was true hundreds of years ago. House builders today have learned much from house builders who lived long ago.

Then

Long ago the Anasazi (Ahn uh SAH zee) built homes under cliffs. They made homes with mud bricks and stones. The thick walls kept the house cool. The roof of one home could become the patio, or outdoor yard, of the house above it.

Now Many families live in apartment buildings. The walls are thick to keep out very hot or very cold weather. Apartments today are made with metal, glass, and brick. Many buildings have balconies and patios.

Think About It!

1 Look at the two pictures. How are the shelters alike? How are they different?

2 **Think About the Future** How do you think people will build homes in the future? Draw your ideas and share them with a friend.

Colonists Build a New Nation

Main Idea Colonists fought a war with Great Britain to make a new country in North America.

More people moved to America from Europe and Africa. The British, French, and Spanish all started colonies in America. Africans were forced to come to the colonies to work for others. There were 13 British colonies along the east coast, near the Atlantic Ocean.

Everyone in the family had a job. Women taught young girls to sew, sweep, and cook. Boys worked with their fathers chopping wood, hunting, and planting.

Many children in the colonies learned school lessons from their mothers. Other children went to schools set up by women in their homes. Many girls did not go to school at all.

Colonists who lived on farms tried to make everything they needed. Sometimes they needed things they could not make. People had to depend on others for their needs.

The blacksmith used iron to make tools such as hoes and hammers. The cooper shaped barrels and water buckets from wood. Every family used barrels to store things.

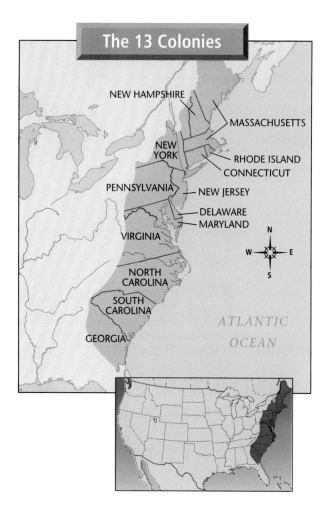

The 13 Colonies

Unfair Taxes

The 13 colonies were ruled by King George of Great Britain. British lawmakers made laws and taxes for the colonies. A **tax** is money we pay to a country, state, or town for things communities need, such as roads. The colonists had to pay taxes on goods they bought from Great Britain, such as tea and printed paper.

The colonists thought some of these taxes and laws were unfair, because they had no say in making them. Some colonists did not want to be ruled by Great Britain at all. They wanted their freedom. **Freedom** is being able to act and make choices for yourself.

The Stamp Act put a tax on printed papers.

The Fight for Freedom

Samuel Adams, a Massachusetts leader, believed in freedom. He wrote letters and talked to other Americans. He wanted to free the colonies from the rule of Great Britain. Many colonists agreed with Adams. They gathered in groups to talk about freedom.

On April 19, 1775, people stopped talking and began fighting for freedom. In the colony of Massachusetts, farmers fought British soldiers on the roads and in the fields. When Sam Adams heard about the fighting he said,

"Oh! what a glorious morning is this!"

That was the beginning of the war between the American colonists and Great Britain. We call that war the Revolutionary War or the American Revolution.

Samuel Adams

On July 4, 1776, the American leaders signed a paper that said they wanted their freedom from Great Britain. It was written by Thomas Jefferson. The paper is called the Declaration of Independence. Every Fourth of July we remember how the colonies fought to be free from the rule of Great Britain.

The war lasted five more years. George Washington led the American army. Many men, women, and children worked hard to free the colonies from Great Britain. Some women, like Molly Pitcher, fought too. When her husband was hurt, Molly Pitcher took his place firing a cannon.

When the Revolutionary War was over, the colonies were free. Americans called their new nation the United States of America. There were many choices to make for the new country. How would all the states work together? What laws would there be?

Leaders from all the states met to talk about their ideas. They voted for the first President of the United States. When people **vote** they make a choice. They chose George Washington to be President of the new country.

George Washington

George Washington gave badges to soldiers who fought well.

What Did You Learn?

1 **Key Words:** Write these words in sentences to show their meaning: **tax, freedom**.

2 What is the Declaration of Independence?

3 Write about or draw a picture that describes some of the jobs people had in the colonies.

Making Predictions

Have you ever looked outside on a cloudy day? When the clouds turn dark, what will happen next? You might predict rain. Predicting means using what you know to think about what will happen next.

When you read, you can use what you already know and words and picture clues to help you make predictions. Predicting helps you understand better what you are reading. By reading on, you can check your prediction.

❶ Here's How

Look at the title and the first paragraph on page 141.

- Read the paragraph that follows the title. What clues help you predict what Phillis Wheatley may do when she is older?

- How could you check your prediction?

An Early American Writer

Phillis Wheatley was born in Africa. When she was about seven years old she was brought to the United States with other Africans as a slave. She worked without pay for the Wheatley family. Phillis Wheatley taught herself to read and write.

She liked to write poems. During the American Revolution, George Washington was an important general. Phillis Wheatley did something special to honor him.

② Use the Skill

Read the story above about Phillis Wheatley and answer the questions below.

1. What do you predict Phillis will do to honor George Washington?

2. What clues helped you make your prediction?

3. Share you prediction with a friend. Is it the same or different?

LESSON 4

Settlers on the Move

Main Idea Settlers moved from the East across America to make new homes.

Key Word

pioneer

After the Revolutionary War, the United States grew fast. As the country grew, people wanted more land and resources. American explorers wanted to map the continent. With good maps, people could find ways to move west.

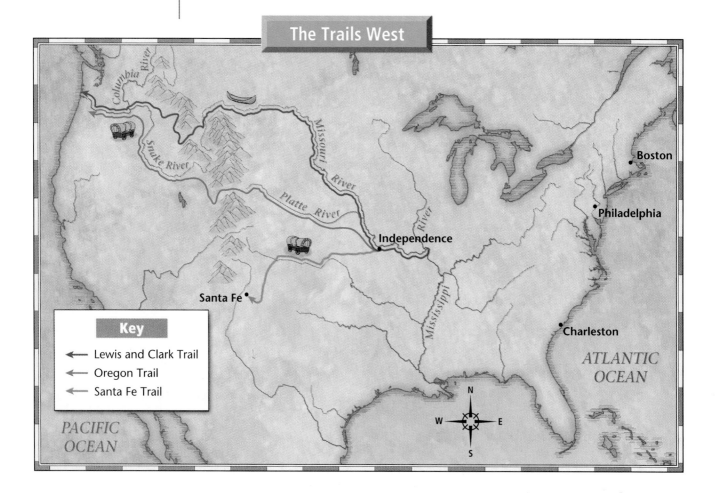

The Trails West

Key

← Lewis and Clark Trail
← Oregon Trail
← Santa Fe Trail

Columbia River

Snake River

Missouri River

Platte River

Mississippi River

Independence

Santa Fe

Boston

Philadelphia

Charleston

ATLANTIC OCEAN

PACIFIC OCEAN

N W E S

142

Merriweather Lewis and William Clark led a group of explorers across the continent to the Pacific Ocean. A Shoshone woman named Sacagawea (sak uh juh WEE uh) helped them find their way. The explorers brought back stories of rich soil, fresh water, and beautiful land.

People from the East heard the stories. They packed their things and moved west in covered wagons. They were pioneers. A **pioneer** is someone who does something first and leads the way for other people.

Thousands of pioneers wanted their own land to farm. At first they settled where Ohio, Kentucky, and Tennessee are today. Then some families traveled farther in groups called wagon trains. You can see some of the trails the wagons followed on the map on page 142.

Life on the Trail

The wagon train might travel 10 miles in one day. At the end of each day, the families formed a circle with their wagons. Children gathered wood to make fires for cooking and to keep warm.

Camping on the trail

Life on the trail could be hard. The sun was hot and there was no shade on the plains. Fresh water could also be a problem. Sometimes it was hard to find. People got sick and died. Others were swept away while crossing fast moving rivers.

Changes for Native Americans

Native Americans lived in communities all across the United States. Some pioneers built homes and settled on Native American land. Many Native Americans fought to protect their communities. The United States sent soldiers and forced Native American groups to move onto land that the pioneers did not want. These lands were called reservations.

What Did You Learn?

1. **Key Word:** Write a sentence using the word **pioneer**.

2. Why did people move from the East to the West?

3. Write a sentence to tell what happened to Native Americans when pioneers moved west.

Identifying Boundaries

Maps show boundaries. A boundary tells where one area ends and another one begins. Boundaries are between two places, such as a country or a state.

A boundary can be natural like a river. A boundary can also be a line that separates two places, such as the line where your yard ends and a neighbor's begins.

Minnesota Boundaries

Key
— National boundary
— State boundary

1 Here's How

Look at this map.

- Find the Mississippi River. It is a natural boundary. What states does it separate from Iowa?

- Is the boundary between Minnesota and Iowa natural or human-made?

- Look at the map key. Why is one boundary line of Minnesota thicker than the others?

Boundaries of the United States

CANADA

WASHINGTON

Columbia R.

OREGON

MONTANA

IDAHO

WYOMING

NORTH DAKOTA

SOUTH DAKOTA

MINNESOTA

Lake Superior

WISCONSIN

MICHIGAN

Lake Huron

Lake Ontario

MAINE

VERMONT

NEW HAMPSHIRE
MASSACHUSETTS

NEW YORK

RHODE ISLAND
CONNECTICUT

PENNSYLVANIA

NEW JERSEY

NEVADA

UTAH

River

COLORADO

KANSAS

NEBRASKA

IOWA

Missouri

Mississippi

ILLINOIS

INDIANA

OHIO

River

WEST VIRGINIA

DELAWARE

MARYLAND

VIRGINIA

CALIFORNIA

Colorado

MISSOURI

Ohio

KENTUCKY

ARIZONA

NEW MEXICO

OKLAHOMA

Red River

ARKANSAS

TENNESSEE

NORTH CAROLINA

SOUTH CAROLINA

GEORGIA

ALABAMA

MISSISSIPPI

LOUISIANA

FLORIDA

ATLANTIC OCEAN

N
W E
S

TEXAS

Rio Grande

PACIFIC OCEAN

MEXICO

GULF OF MEXICO

Key

— National boundary
— State boundary

2 Use the Skill

Look at the map above to answer the questions.

1. Find Missouri. Pretend you are a pioneer. You travel from Missouri to Colorado. How many state boundaries do you cross?

2. Name three states that have the Mississippi River as one of their natural boundaries.

3. Name two states that have national boundary lines.

Our Nation Changes

Main Idea Life in America changed because of new ideas about fairness.

Most people agree that people should be treated fairly. At one time, however, the United States allowed **slavery**. It was a cruel, unfair system in which people were forced to work for others without pay. They were not free to leave, to go to school, or to live as they wanted. Many African people, called slaves, were forced to do hard work.

Some people thought slavery was wrong. Frederick Douglass was a slave. He ran away to be free. Then Douglass gave speeches about how unfair slavery was. Two sisters, Sarah and Angelina Grimké, also spoke out against slavery. They were some of the first women to speak about this in public.

Frederick Douglass

Key

	The North
	The South
	Territories
	Free States

The Civil War

Some farmers in the South used slaves to work their farms. These states wanted to keep slavery. They did not want others to tell them what to do. Some southern states broke away from the United States to form their own country.

This started the Civil War. President Abraham Lincoln wanted all the states in the North and the South to stay together as one country. He promised to end slavery. After four years of war, the South gave up. All the states became one country again. The slaves were freed.

Abraham Lincoln

149

America Changes

Immigrants at Ellis Island

After the Civil War many new immigrants came to the United States. An **immigrant** is a person who moves from one country to another to live. Immigrants came to the United States from countries in Asia, Europe, Central and South America.

Immigrants came for many reasons. Some left their countries to find jobs so they could feed their families. Others hoped to be treated fairly by their leaders.

Coming to America was not easy. Immigrants from Europe and Asia sailed in crowded ships with their belongings. Families from Mexico walked for many days to reach the United States.

Many immigrants came from Europe. They stopped at Ellis Island in New York harbor. Immigrants from Asia stopped at Angel Island in California. Immigrants had to answer many questions and wait a long time to enter the United States.

Immigrants at Angel Island

Life in America was hard for immigrants. Many did not speak English. It was hard to find work. Some Americans did not treat the immigrants fairly because they seemed different.

Alexander Graham Bell

Immigrants helped the United States in many ways. They brought new ideas from their countries. Alexander Graham Bell, from Scotland, invented the first telephone. Lue Gim Gon, from China, found a way to grow a new kind of orange. Most immigrants worked hard. They helped make the country better.

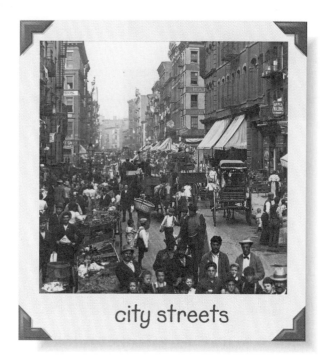
city streets

As more and more immigrants moved to the United States, cities became more crowded. Americans moved to cities to find new jobs. Some African Americans left farms in the South to work in cities in the North.

Men and women found jobs in factories. Even children had to work. Many did not go to school. Factories were dangerous. Some workers got hurt or sick. People worked for many hours without food or water. Many factories had no heat in the winter and the windows did not open in the summer.

child working in a factory

You read that slavery was unfair. Abraham Lincoln and others worked to end it. The work in factories was not as bad as slavery, but workers were not treated fairly. People passed laws to make things better for workers and children.

People from all over the world have changed the United States. They made it a better place to live. People still work to make fair laws for all people. How is your life different from the lives of children long ago?

Children in school

What Did You Learn?

1. **Key Words:** Define the word **immigrant**.
2. What did people do to change the way factories treated workers?
3. Write about one person you read about. How did that person change our country?

Reading Timelines

A timeline is an ordered group of pictures, words, and dates that shows when events happened. A timeline is marked in equal parts. Each part shows the same length of time.

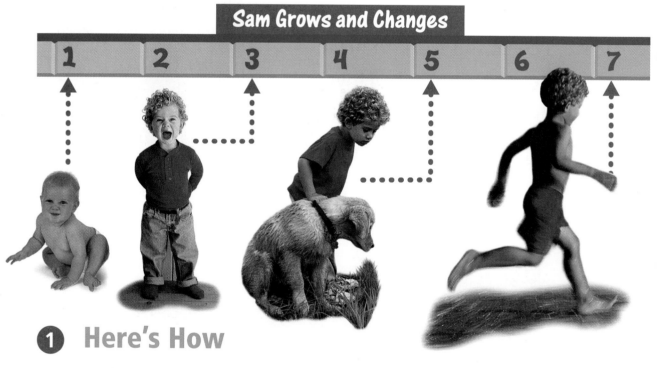

Sam Grows and Changes

1   2   3   4   5   6   7

❶ Here's How

- What is the title of the timeline above?

- What are the first and last numbers on the timeline? Each number stands for a year in Sam's life. The events on the timeline happened between these years.

- When did Sam and his dog go exploring?

154

People Who Changed America

1880	1900	1920

1879
Thomas Edison and a team of scientists invent a light bulb that can burn for longer than any light bulb before it.

1903
Wilbur and Orville Wright make four flights in an airplane powered by an engine. The first flight lasts 12 seconds. The fourth flight lasts 59 seconds.

1923
George Washington Carver gets a medal for his research. He found ways to make more than 300 products from peanuts and sweet potatoes.

❷ Use the Skill

1. What is the timeline about?

2. When did George Washington Carver get a medal?

3. What did the Wright brothers do in 1903?

155

When I First Came to This Land

Words and Music by Oscar Brand

Simply

When I first came to this land, I was not a
wealth-y man. Then I built my-self a
shack, I did what I could. *(fine)* I

After verse one, repeat as necessary

called my shack, Break-my-back. I

Chorus *D.S. al fine* *Repeat*

Still the land was sweet and good, I did what I could.

When I first came to this land,
I was not a wealthy man.
Then I bought myself a cow,
I did what I could.
I called my cow,
No-milk-now. *(Repeat last line of verse one)*
Chorus

When I first came to this land,
I was not a wealthy man.
Then I bought myself a horse,
I did what I could.
I called my horse,
Lame-of-course. *(Repeat last lines of verses one and two)*
Chorus

When I first came to this land,
I was not a wealthy man.
Then I bought myself a duck,
I did what I could.
I called my duck,
Out-of-luck. *(Repeat last lines of verses one, two, and three)*
Chorus

Response Activity

Make a list of rhyming words from
the song.

Theme 4
Review

Theme 4 Big Ideas

1. Write or say one thing you learned about the pictures below.

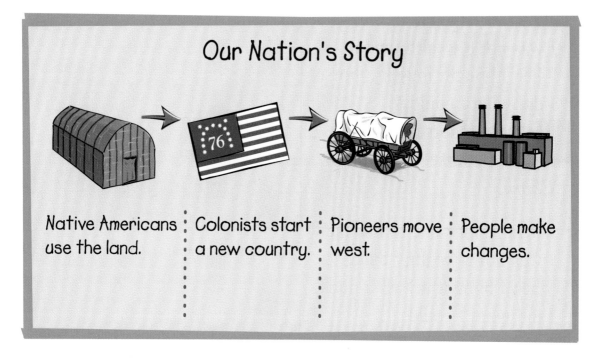

Our Nation's Story

Native Americans use the land. : Colonists start a new country. : Pioneers move west. : People make changes.

Review What You Learned

2. What are some of the foods the Muscogee and the Kwakiutl ate?

3. How did Squanto help the Pilgrims?

4. Why did the American colonists think the British tax laws were unfair?

5. What was a wagon train?

6. What ended after the Civil War?

Use the key words below to complete the sentences.

colonist (p. 130)   immigrant (p. 150)

explorer (p. 126)   pioneer (p. 143)

history (p. 122)   vote (p.139)

7.   The story of the past is called _____.

8.   A _____ is a settler who moves to a
     colony, a place that is ruled by another
     country.

9.   Christopher Columbus was an _____.

10. A _____ is a person who does something
     first and leads the way for other people.

11. Americans _____ to choose their leaders.

12. An _____ is a person who moves from
     one country to another.

Write a Story

13. Pretend you lived long ago. Write
     a story about what you did for
     one day. You could be a Native
     American, a colonist, a pioneer,
     or an immigrant.

     • Where do you live?

     • What is your job?

     • How do you use the natural
       resources around you?

My Day On the Trail

Today, my family got on the wagon. We left early in the morning. It was still dark. Our wagon followed other wagons.

159

Use the timeline to answer the questions below.

14. What is the timeline about?

15. Who came first, the Pilgrims or the soldiers at St. Augustine?

People Come to America

1400	1500	1600

In 1492, Columbus sails to the Americas.

In 1565, Spain sends soldiers to St. Augustine.

In 1620, Pilgrims settle in Plymouth.

Read the story in the box to answer the question.

16. Predict who was chosen as President. What clues helped you predict?

Use the map to answer these questions.

17. What is a natural boundary between Mississippi and Louisiana?

18. What state boundary is west of Alabama?

A New President

After the American Revolution, our new nation needed a President. George Washington had led the colonial army during the war. Many people liked him. He was a good general.

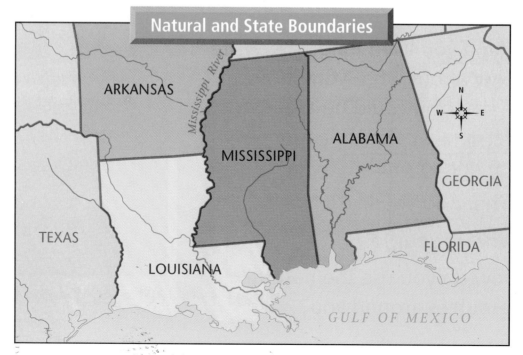

Natural and State Boundaries

ARKANSAS

Mississippi River

TEXAS

MISSISSIPPI

ALABAMA

GEORGIA

LOUISIANA

FLORIDA

GULF OF MEXICO

Put on an American History Play

1. Work in small groups. List some of the groups of people you learned about in this theme and what they did. You might have a Kwakiutl family building a canoe or a pioneer family traveling in a covered wagon.

2. Choose one from your list for a play.

3. List ideas for a *beginning, middle,* and *end* for your play. Choose parts.

4. Make costumes and props.

5. Present your play. Have everyone make up words as they go along.

Things You'll Need

- old clothes for costumes
- construction paper
- glue
- scissors
- markers

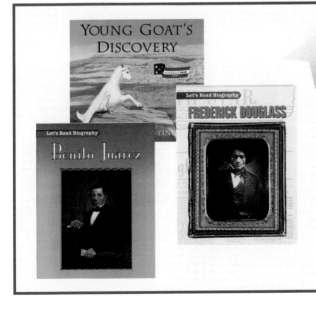

Read On Your Own

Young Goat's Discovery
by Arline Warner Tinus

Let's Read Biography:
Frederick Douglass

Let's Read Biography:
Benito Juárez

America's People

The night is beautiful,
So the faces of my people.

The stars are beautiful,
So the eyes of my people.

Beautiful, also, is the sun.
Beautiful, also, are the souls of my people.

"My People" by Langston Hughes

Key Words

ancestor	relative	tradition

Lesson 1, page 164	Lesson 1, page 164	Lesson 2, page 174

holiday

Lesson 2, page 175

hero

Lesson 3, page 180

contribution

Lesson 3, page 180

LESSON 1

Family Stories, Past and Present

Main Idea You can learn about your culture, your family, and yourself through family stories.

Key Words

ancestor
relative

People in the United States today have ancestors from all over the world. An **ancestor** is someone in your family who lived before you.

You can learn from your ancestors and your relatives. A **relative** is a person who is part of your family today. Your relatives share their language and ways of doing things. They teach you what they think is important. Relatives tell you what rules to follow and how to treat others.

164

Different Families, Different Stories

Millions of different families live in the United States. Some families are very large. Others are small. You may know many or only a few of your relatives.

American families come from many cultures. They have many ideas and ways of doing things. These different families make our country a special place to live.

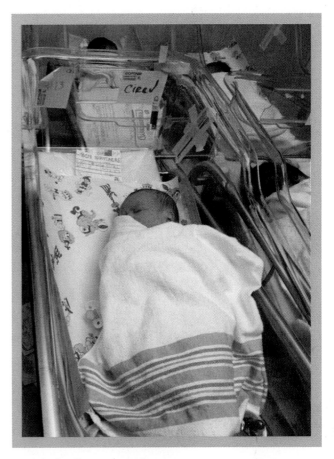

Your father may know a story about the day you were born.

Your grandmother may tell you a story about when she was a little girl.

Family stories tell the history of a family. You can learn about your ancestors, your relatives, and yourself from your family stories. They help you learn what is important to your relatives. Then you can decide what is important to you.

Meet Kirstin's Family

Kirstin Hoogendoorn lives in Ohio. Her mother's ancestors came from France, Scotland, and Germany. Her great-great-grandfather was a Cherokee. Her father's parents are from the Netherlands.

The Netherlands

Kirstin is learning about her Dutch culture from her grandfather, Opa. He teaches Kirstin how to speak some Dutch words. On the evening of December 5, her family celebrates Sinter Klaas. Kirstin likes getting presents on this day. She is proud of her ancestors.

On Sinter Klaas, Kirstin gets a chocolate H, the first letter of her last name.

Meet the Lee Family

Jessa, Julia, and Ryan Lee live in California. Their mother's ancestors came from Japan. Their father's ancestors are from China. The children are learning customs and languages from both parents.

The Lee children go to a special Japanese culture program every summer. Jessa and Julia have also taken Chinese language classes.

Japan

China

Children get a red envelope filled with money on the Chinese New Year.

The Lee children have two different New Year celebrations. On January 1, they celebrate with their mother's family and eat omochi (oh moh chee), a Japanese food. On the Chinese New Year, which falls later in the year, they celebrate with their father's family.

167

Meet Gabriel's Family

Gabriel Lafontant lives in Massachusetts. His father came to the United States from the island of Haiti when he was 17. He came here to go to college.

Mr. Lafontant had to learn English when he came. He is teaching Gabriel how to speak the French and Creole languages. Gabriel celebrates Haiti's Independence Day on January 1 with his father.

Haiti

This is the flag of the Republic of Haiti.

Gabriel loves to visit his grandmother in Haiti. He enjoys the warm weather there and the tasty food his grandmother makes. His grandmother helps take care of her relatives and neighbors. She is teaching Gabriel how to be kind to others.

You have now met three families in the United States. There are millions of other families. Each one is special. Each one has its own stories. Together, these stories become part of America's story.

What stories have you learned about your family? Do you hear stories about your relatives? What do you like best about these stories?

What Did You Learn?

1. **Key Words:** Use **ancestor** and **relative** in sentences that show what the words mean.

2. What are two things you can learn from your relatives?

3. Write a family story.

Why Do People Move?

People move around in the United States. Maybe you have moved from another school, city, or state. Many people have moved to the United States from other countries.

People move for many reasons. Some move to find a new job or to be closer to their families. Others look for more space or a different kind of weather. Sometimes, people move to a new country to find safety. There may be fighting in their own country.

Math Connection

Once people moved to this country by sailing ships or steamships. Today, people can move more quickly by airplane. Look at the picture. What is the fastest way to travel from China to the United States?

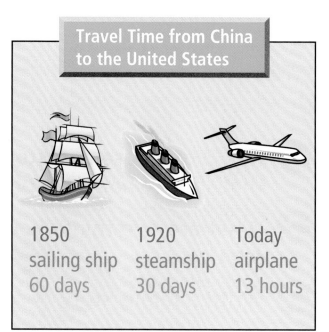

Travel Time from China to the United States

1850	1920	Today
sailing ship	steamship	airplane
60 days	30 days	13 hours

170

Work

People often move to find a new job.

Family

Some people move to live closer to their relatives.

Weather

Sometimes people move to a place that has different weather.

Think About It!

1. Look at the pictures above. What are two reasons why people move?

2. Where would you like to move? Find the place on a map and draw a picture of it.

171

Reading a Bar Graph

You see a bowl of fruit on a table. Someone asks you if there are more apples, oranges, or bananas. How could you quickly show this to a friend? Making a bar graph can help.

A bar graph uses bars to show how much there is of different groups of items. You make one bar for each group. Look at all the bars to compare. The title tells you what the bar graph compares. The numbers on the side of the graph tell you how many are in each group.

❶ Here's How

Look at the bar graph.

- What does this bar graph compare?

- How many oranges are there?

- Which bar shows the most fruit? How can you tell?

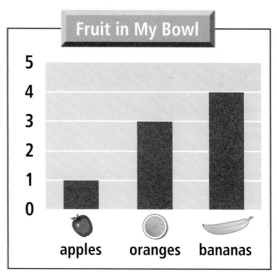

Fruit in My Bowl

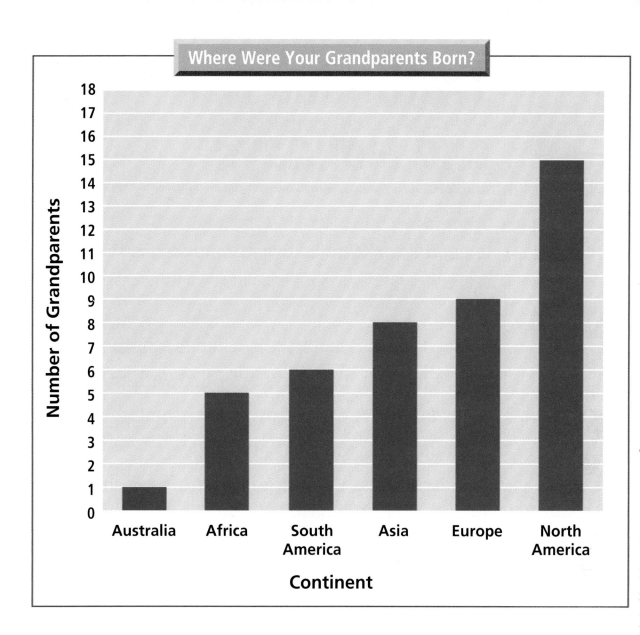

Where Were Your Grandparents Born?

 Use the Skill

1. Look for the tallest bar. Where were the grandparents born?

2. How many grandparents were born in North America?

3. Look for the smallest bar. Where were the grandparents born? How many are there?

Traditions and Holidays

Main Idea Traditions and holidays help us remember the events, beliefs, and ideas of our culture.

Jacob loves the birthday cake his mother makes for him. Birthdays are filled with traditions in his family. A **tradition** is something that is done the same way year after year.

Parents pass down traditions to their children. Traditions tell a lot about a family's beliefs, customs, or ideas. You may sing songs, wear special clothes, or eat certain foods.

Blowing out candles is one birthday tradition.

At Passover, Jewish families eat a meal called a Seder. Each food is a symbol of the Passover story.

During Ramadan, Muslims do not eat or drink during the daytime. In the evenings, families have special foods.

On Palm Sunday, many Christians get palm leaves at church. The palms are a symbol of an event long ago.

Holidays Are Special Days

We celebrate our holidays with traditions. A **holiday** is a time that honors a person or celebrates an important event from the past. On holidays, people have traditions that they do every year.

Many people around the world celebrate some religious holidays at the same time. People remember past events on religious holidays. These events are important to their beliefs. Prayers, ceremonies, and foods are part of the traditions of religious holidays.

Community Traditions

Communities sometimes have their own traditions and holidays. Groups of people or whole cities might honor a person, an event, or a culture. The city of Pendleton, South Carolina, has a Spring Jubilee Festival each year. The Jubilee has walking tours of old places and a crafts fair.

Dancing is part of the Spring Jubilee Festival in Pendleton, South Carolina.

This is the state capitol building in Honolulu, Hawaii.

State Holidays

A state can also have a holiday to honor important people or to mark an event. Hawaii became the fiftieth state on August 21, 1959. Each year on the third Friday in August, Hawaii celebrates this event. People in Hawaii call the holiday Admission Day.

National Holidays

Days that are important to our whole nation are national holidays. This is the time we remember important people and events in history. We feel proud of being part of our country.

This picture shows most of our national holidays. Traditional foods and events are often part of national holidays. Many people hang flags outside their homes on the Fourth of July. Some families have picnics and watch fireworks. How do you celebrate national holidays in your community?

National Holidays
★ Martin Luther King, Jr. Day
  Third Monday in January
★ Presidents' Day
  Third Monday in February
★ Memorial Day
  Last Monday in May
★ Independence Day
  July 4
★ Labor Day
  First Monday in September
★ Veterans Day
  November 11
★ Thanksgiving
  Fourth Thursday in November

What Did You Learn?

1. **Key Words:** Write sentences with the words **tradition** and **holiday** to show what they mean.

2. Name a state holiday and a national holiday you learned about in this lesson.

3. Write about a tradition in your family.

Using a Library

You can visit a library to learn more about your state. A library has books, magazines, newspapers, and other ways to get facts. A card catalog or computer catalog gives you the author, title, and subject of all the books in the library.

A library has reference books. They give facts and information about real things. Dictionaries and encyclopedias are reference books. They are organized in ABC order.

① Here's How

Look at the books to the right.

- How could you find these books in a library?

- Which books are reference books?

- What information would you find in a dictionary?

Dictionary

Books

Encyclopedia

ARIZONA

Subject Search Results: Arizona

Arizona A-Z, Dorothy Hines Weaver, 1994.

Arizona Facts and Symbols, Emily McAuliffe, 1998.

**Coyote and the Winnowing Birds:
a Traditional Hopi Tale,** Eugene Sekaquatewa.

Grand Canyon: A Trail Through Time,
Linda Vieira, 1997.

My Great Aunt Arizona, Gloria Houston, 1997.

 Use the Skill

1. What subject do you see on the computer catalog above?

2. Which book on this list might show the Arizona state flag?

3. Which book on the list would help you learn more about the Grand Canyon?

179

LESSON 3

Heroes

Main Idea Heroes are people we honor for their contributions to others.

Key Words

hero
contribution

Our country's history is filled with stories. Many stories are about heroes from the past and the present. A **hero** is a person who does something very special to help others. Heroes work hard to change the way things are. They try to reach the goals they set for themselves.

Heroes from around the world make contributions to our lives. A **contribution** is something you do or give to help others.

180

Jonas Salk

Heroes Do Great Things

Jonas Salk (SAWLK) was a doctor. He liked doing research. He wanted to find ways to stop deadly illnesses. He found a cure for an illness called polio. His work helped save many lives.

Dolores Huerta (WEHR tah) was a teacher. Many of the parents of her students were farm workers. They moved often. She and Cesar Chávez started the United Farm Workers. The group makes sure that farm workers are treated fairly.

Dolores Huerta

Martin Luther King, Jr.

Martin Luther King, Jr., was a minister and a leader. He worked hard to make sure that all Americans are treated fairly. Dr. King found peaceful ways to fight for fair laws for all people.

Heroes Long Ago

Hatshepsut (haht SHEHP soot) was a great ruler in Egypt thousands of years ago. Few rulers were women at that time. She helped make Egypt a rich and peaceful place.

Hatshepsut

Aesop

Aesop (AY sahp) was a storyteller who lived in Greece about 2,500 years ago. He collected folktales called fables. These stories teach lessons about life. His fables are still read by people around the world today.

Murasaki Shikibu (moo rah SAH kee SHEE kee boo) lived in Japan about 1,000 years ago. She wrote *The Tale of Genji*. Some people think it is the first novel. It is a story of make-believe people and events.

This is a picture from Murasaki Shikibu's story.

Johannes Gutenberg

Johannes Gutenberg (yoh HAH nehz GOOT n burg) was a German printer. He invented a new kind of printing press almost 600 years ago. Before this time, people in Europe copied books by hand. His invention made it faster and cheaper to print books.

Teachers, parents, and other family members can be heroes, too. Heroes show us how to work hard and make contributions. Who are your heroes?

What Did You Learn?

1. **Key Words:** Define **hero** and **contribution.**
2. Name three heroes you learned about in this lesson.
3. Write about one of your own heroes. Share what you wrote with a friend.

Taking a Survey

You can find out about your friends' heroes in history. One way to find out information is to take a survey. A survey is a question or set of questions that you ask many different people to find out what they think about something. You might be surprised at all the different answers you get to the same question.

① Here's How

- Write a question to find out who are your classmates' heroes from history. Then ask your classmates the question.

- How will you keep track of your friends' answers? Look at the next page for one idea.

- What do you think you will learn?

Who is one of your heroes in history?

George Washington	|||
Martin Luther King, Jr.	⦀⦀ (5)
Molly Pitcher	||
Abraham Lincoln	⦀⦀ | (6)
Frederick Douglass	⦀⦀ | (6)
Dolores Huerta	|||

② Use the Skill

Take another survey.

1. Make up a question for the survey. It should ask your classmates to name a hero who is alive today.

2. Write the names. Use tallies to keep track of how many people choose each hero.

3. Look at the tallies. What did you learn from your survey?

Our Family Comes from 'Round the World

by Mary Ann Hoberman

Our family comes
From 'round the world.
Our hair is straight,
Our hair is curled,
Our eyes are brown,
Our eyes are blue,
Our skins are different
Colors, too.

Tra la tra la
Tra la tra lee
We're one big happy family!

We're girls and boys,
We're big and small,
We're young and old,
We're short and tall.
We're everything
That we can be
And still we are
A family.

86

O la dee da
O la dee dee
We're one big happy family!

We laugh and cry,
We work and play,
We help each other
Every day.
The world's a lovely
Place to be
Because we are
A family.

Hurray hurrah
Hurrah hurree
We're one big happy family!

Response Activity

Write a poem about your classroom family. Write about the ways you are alike and the ways you are different.

187

Theme 5
Review

Theme 5 Big Ideas

1. Write something you learned about each of the pictures below.

America's People

Ancestors and Family Stories

Holidays and Traditions

Heroes

Review What You Learned

2. What can you learn from family stories?

3. What is a community tradition in Pendleton, South Carolina?

4. What are two national holidays that people celebrate in the United States?

5. Who was Johannes Gutenberg?

Use the key words below to fill in the sentences.

ancestor (p. 164)   holiday (p. 175)

contribution (p. 180)   relative (p. 164)

hero (p. 180)   tradition (p. 174)

6. George Washington made an important _____ to our country.

7. A _____ is a person who is part of your family today.

8. Jonas Salk is a _____ because he helped many people.

9. Your great-grandmother is an _____.

10. Birthday cakes are a _____ for some families.

11. School is closed on a national _____.

Write a Report

12. Write a one-page report about a hero. Pick someone you know or someone from history who is a hero. Answer these questions in your report.

   • Why is this person a hero to you?

   • What contributions has this hero made?

   • How has your hero worked to change something or to achieve a goal?

My Hero
My grandmother is a hero. She is a great person. She lives in my house. She takes care of me and my brother. She works really hard. I hope I can be like her when I grow up.

One class made a bar graph. It shows who has moved in their class and from where they moved. Use the bar graph to answer these questions.

13. How many children have moved within the United States?

14. Which group is the largest?

15. Which group is the smallest?

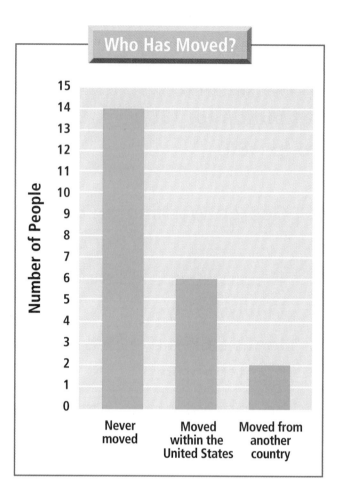

Who Has Moved?

Number of People

Never moved | Moved within the United States | Moved from another country

Use the skills you have learned to answer the questions.

16. Name two kinds of reference books you can find in a library.

17. What can you use to find books in a library?

18. What steps do you follow to take a survey?

Our Many Cultures Display

Things You'll Need
- paper
- markers
- reference books

1 Choose a culture to learn about. It can be your own culture or one that interests you.

2 Find books at the library. Find out how people lived in the past and how they live today. Look for pictures, maps, flags, recipes, and songs.

3 Talk to people about old and new family stories, celebrations, and traditions.

4 Display your information on a bulletin board, in a scrapbook, or in some other display.

Read On Your Own

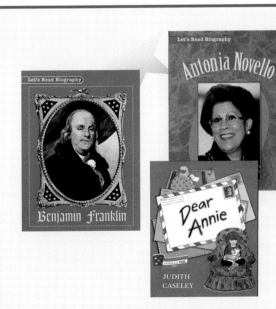

Let's Read Biography:
Antonia Novello

Let's Read Biography:
Benjamin Franklin

Dear Annie
By Judith Caseley

Theme 6

Our Government

My country 'tis of thee,
Sweet land of liberty,
Of thee I sing.

from the song "America"
words by Samuel Francis Smith
music attributed to Henry Carey

Key Words

government	mayor	President

Lesson 1, page 195	Lesson 1, page 196	Lesson 2, page 202

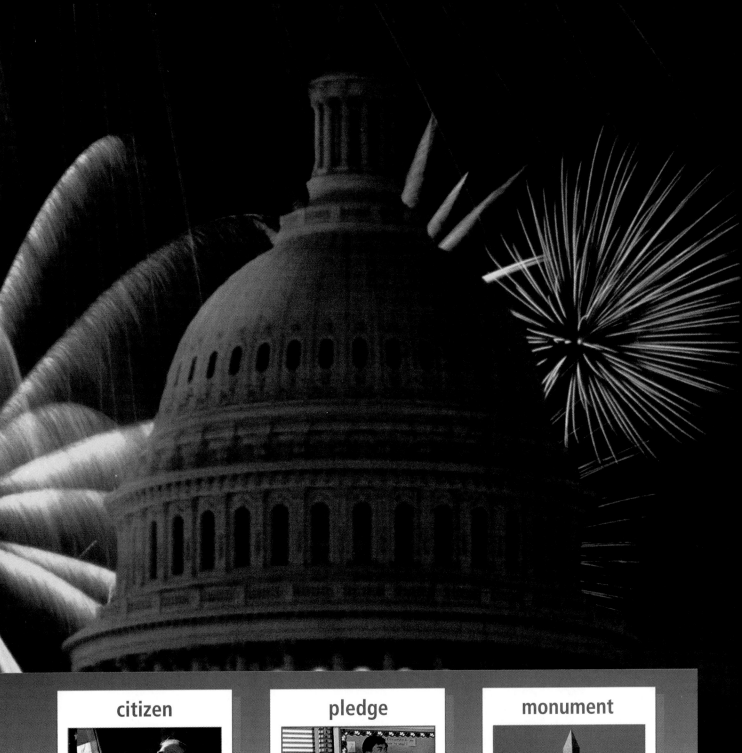

citizen

Lesson 3, page 206

pledge

Lesson 3, page 207

monument

Lesson 4, page 212

Rules and Laws

Main Idea Your community and your state have a government.

Key Words

government
election
mayor
city council
governor

A group of friends wanted to start a pet club. One day, they tried to make plans.

"When will the club meet?" asked Beth.

"Who can join the club?" asked Luke.

"I want to be in charge." said Shawna.

The club had no rules to keep order. They needed a leader to help. How could the children work together?

The club needed a government. A **government** is a group of people who work together to bring order to a community, state, or nation. A government could help the Pet Club, too.

To keep order, governments make laws. You learned that laws help people live together. Lawmakers and community leaders can make laws to keep people safe or to care for schools and parks.

In many places, people vote for their government leaders. An **election** is a time when people vote to choose their leaders. People vote for leaders whom they believe will make fair laws and good choices.

Local Government

The city or town you live in has a government. The leader in most communities is called a **mayor** or a town manager. A small group of people called the **city council** helps the mayor run the local government. Communities hold elections to vote for these leaders.

There are many other people in local government who help run your city or town. In some communities the mayor picks the leaders to help. In other places, these leaders are elected. Who are the leaders in your local government?

Our Community Government

Mayor

City Council

Police Chief

Fire Chief

Superintendent of Roads

Superintendent of Parks and Grounds

State Government

Your state has a government, too. The leader of a state is called a **governor**. The state government does many different things for the people who live in the state. It takes care of state roads and parks. States also make laws about health, driving, safety, and transportation.

This is the governor of South Carolina.

How did the Pet Club members make their own government? They elected a leader and made a list of rules. Now their club can run more smoothly.

What Did You Learn?

1 **Key Words:** Write these words in sentences to show what they mean: **mayor** and **city council**.

2 How do people choose a mayor or a governor?

3 Write about two jobs in a town or city government.

Reading a Chart

A chart can help you order and compare information. When you list facts in a chart, it is easier to see them. Then the facts are easier to compare.

A chart has columns and rows. You read a column from top to bottom. You read a row from left to right. The titles at the top of the columns tell what information appears on the chart.

Our Pets		
Name	Cat	Dog
Luke	0	2
Shawna	1	1
Beth	1	0

 **1** **Here's How**

Look at the chart.

- Read the title of the chart. What is it about?

- What are the titles of the columns? What are the titles of the rows?

- Read the column marked **Cat**. How many cats do these friends have in all?

- Read across the row marked **Beth**. Does she have a cat or a dog? How do you know?

Police Cars and Fire Engines

Town Name	Police Cars	Fire Engines
Franklin	10	4
Clarksville	2	1
Hillsdale	5	2
Oakmount	7	5
Ballston	1	0
Henderson	3	3

2 Use the Skill

1. What is this chart about?

2. How many towns are shown on this chart?

3. Which town has the most police cars?
   Which town has the fewest fire engines?

Our Nation's Government

Main Idea The Constitution describes the United States government.

How do you make a government for a country? About 200 years ago, American leaders came to the city of Philadelphia, Pennsylvania. They came to plan a new government for the United States.

The leaders talked about ways to run the new country. It was hard work. The plan they wrote is called the Constitution of the United States.

Liberty means freedom.

Justice means fair laws.

Equality means people have the same rights.

The Constitution

The Constitution tells how our country's government works. It lists important laws that protect people's freedoms, or rights. It says that all people in the United States should be treated fairly.

The Constitution also says that Americans are free to say or write their own ideas. People are free to pray the way they want. They also have the right to privacy. That means they do not have to show or tell everything to other people. These freedoms are the rights of all people in the United States.

The President

The Constitution says that the United States government has three equal parts that work together. One part is led by the President. The **President** of the United States is the leader of the country. Sometimes the President travels to meet with leaders of other countries. The President can choose people to help run parts of the government. The President lives and works in the White House.

The White House, Washington, D.C.

The Congress

The **Congress** makes laws for the United States. The Senate and the House of Representatives are the two parts of Congress. People in the 50 states vote for the members of Congress. The members listen to the voters in their state. The Congress meets in the Capitol Building.

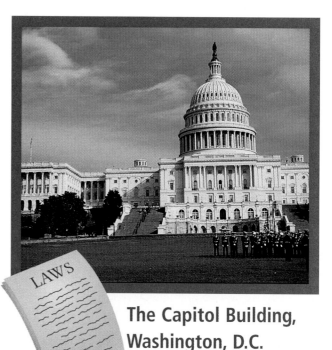

The Capitol Building, Washington, D.C.

The Supreme Court

The Supreme Court Building, Washington, D.C.

The **Supreme Court** has nine judges. A **judge** is the person who makes important decisions in a court of law. The Supreme Court makes sure that all the laws in the country follow the Constitution. The laws must be fair to all people. The judges meet in the Supreme Court Building.

The Constitution is over 200 years old, but it still brings order to our country today. How does the Constitution help you and all people who live in the United States?

What Did You Learn?

1 **Key Words:** Write these words in sentences to show their meaning: **President, Congress, Supreme Court**.

2 What does the Constitution say about people's freedoms in the United States?

3 Write about why you think it is important for all Americans to be treated fairly.

Getting Along

How do you get along with your friends when you disagree? Sometimes you have to compromise. This means that everyone gives up something in order to make things work better for all.

American Leaders Compromise

In 1787, leaders like James Madison met to make a plan for the new government. Different people wanted different things. They made many compromises. They each gave up some things they wanted.

The leaders wrote the Constitution of the United States. It set up a strong government. Some people worried that the government would be too strong.

So the leaders compromised again. They added the Bill of Rights to the Constitution. It lists ten freedoms promised to people in the United States. The government gave up some power so that people could have more freedom.

Share computers on
Mondays and Wednesdays.

Start a computer club
that meets before school.

Divide the class into
two groups.

You Take Action

1 Think of something your class disagrees
about. Some people may want to play
outside. Others want to use the computers.

2 Form two teams. Each team should choose a
side and list what it wants. Then list things
you would be willing to give up.

3 Come back together. Try to find ways to
compromise.

★ Tips for Getting Along ★

- Listen carefully to what others say. They
  might teach you something new.

- Look for a way to change your mind just a
  little. Then ask the others to change their
  minds a little, too.

Being a Good Citizen

Main Idea There are things everyone can do to be a good citizen.

You are a citizen of your town or city. You are also a citizen of your state and country. A **citizen** is a person who belongs to a community or a country.

The United States has many citizens. People from other countries who want to become American citizens ask the government for permission. They must pass a test about United States history and laws.

New citizens at a special ceremony

206

People become American citizens at a special ceremony. They say the "Pledge of Allegiance."

When citizens say the pledge, they promise to be loyal to the United States. A **pledge** is a promise. Allegiance means loyalty.

The pledge says that this country is indivisible. That means it cannot be divided. It is always one nation.

When do you say the "Pledge of Allegiance?"

The Pledge of Allegiance

I pledge allegiance to the flag of the United States of America, and to the Republic for which it stands, one Nation under God, indivisible, with liberty and justice for all.

As a citizen you have responsibilities to your community. A **responsibility** is something that you should do. Your responsibility might be to clean up your room or to help a younger child find the bus.

Citizens also have a responsibility to their country. Citizens who are over 18 years old should vote in elections. Voting lets them choose their leaders. It is a right as well as a responsibility.

Good citizens can be any age. You can do your part to keep the land and water clean. You can follow the rules and laws of your home, school, town, and country. You can also be a good citizen by learning about your community and your government.

What Did You Learn?

1 **Key Words:** Define the words **citizen** and **responsibility**.

2 Why do people say the "Pledge of Allegiance?"

3 Write a "Pledge of Allegiance" for your school.

Do Your Part

From the Pages of

50 SIMPLE THINGS KIDS CAN DO TO SAVE THE EARTH

The EarthWorks Group

The average American uses seven trees a year in paper, wood, and other products used from trees. That's over one and a half billion trees a year.

If every person in the U.S. planted a couple of seeds, there would soon be more than 250 million more plants growing and making the Earth a healthier place to live.

If everyone in the U.S. recycled their Sunday newspapers (including the comics), we'd save 500,000 trees a week.

Response Activity

Keep a tally of how many times you use water each day. Make a chart to show it.

How Can Laws Save a River?

The environment is the natural world around us. For a long time, people did not worry about keeping the environment clean. Factories and cars filled the air with smoke and dirt. People threw waste into rivers.

So people asked the national government to help. Laws to take care of the environment were passed in the 1970s. These laws say that people and factories must keep the environment clean. Now a special group in the national government makes sure these laws and others are followed.

Science Connection

Recycling helps the environment. Many communities have recycling centers. What things do you recycle at home and at school?

← Nashua River
in the 1960s

→ Nashua River
today

Think About It!

1. Look at the photos. Write a sentence that describes how the river looked in the 1960s and how it looks today.

2. Make a list of things that you and your classmates can do to help take care of the environment.

211

Our Nation's Symbols

Main Idea Our nation's symbols remind us of the things that make our country strong.

In the United States we have many symbols that show we are proud of our nation. Some of these symbols are monuments. A **monument** is a statue or a building that is built to remember heroes or important events. You may have monuments in your town.

Key Word

monument

The bald eagle is the national bird of the United States. The bald eagle was chosen because it reminds people of strength and courage.

The Liberty Bell rang out in Philadelphia, Pennsylvania to celebrate the signing of the Declaration of Independence. The bell is a symbol of our country's freedom from Great Britain.

I WANT YOU
for the U.S. ARMY
ENLIST NOW

Uncle Sam is not a real person. He is a symbol of the United States government. Uncle Sam has the same initials as the United States: U.S.

You can see the Washington Monument in Washington, D.C. The monument honors George Washington. He was our first President. Washington is also called the Father of Our Country.

What Did You Learn?

1 **Key Word:** Write **monument** in a sentence to show what it means.

2 What is your favorite American symbol? Write a paragraph to explain why.

Making a Map

Have you ever needed to tell a new friend how to get to your house? Have you ever wanted to show where you went on a trip? These are two times when you could make a map.

When you make a map you need to look carefully at the place you want to map. It helps to take notes about the places you want to show.

map key
□ = house
≈ = road
⬭ = pool

❶ Here's How

Look at the photograph and the map of the neighborhood on the next page.

- What things do you see in the photograph?
- What are the symbols on the map? How do you know?
- Is everything in the correct place on the map? How do you know?

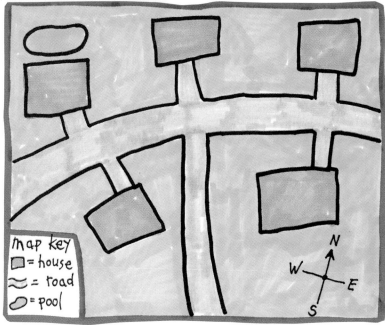

map key
□ = house
≈ = road
⬭ = pool

② Use the Skill

1. Take a walk around your school playground. Take notes about what is there and where everything is.

2. Decide what to show in your map. Make symbols for the map.

3. Draw a map of the playground. Put the symbols you made in the right places. Remember to make a map key.

The Star-Spangled Banner

by Francis Scott Key

Oh say can you see, by the dawn's ear-ly light, What so proud-ly we hailed, at the twi-light's last gleam-ing, Whose broad stripes and bright stars thro' the per-i-lous fight, O'er the ram-parts we watch'd, were so gal-lant-ly stream-ing? And the rock-ets' red glare, the bombs burst-ing in air, Gave

---

dawn — early morning when the sun first comes up

hail — to greet

twilight — the time after sunset

gleaming — shining

perilous — full of danger

rampart — a wall built to protect soldiers from attack

gallantly — brave, courageous

banner — flag

216

proof thro' the night that our flag was still there. Oh,

say, does that_ Star-Spangl - ed Ban - ner_ yet_ wave_ O'er the

land_ of the free and the home of the brave!

Response Activity

Write a paragraph that tells what you think is special about living in the United States of America.

Theme 6 Big Ideas

1. Write or tell how the different parts of the picture below are related.

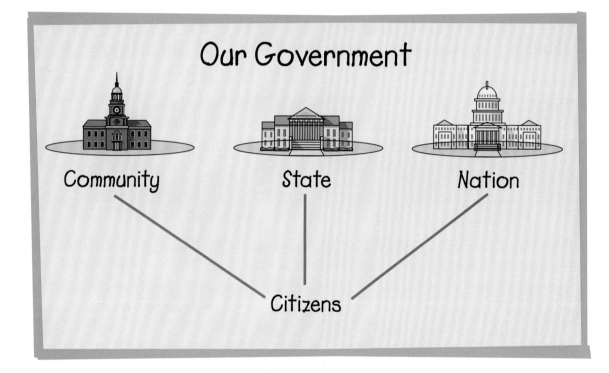

Our Government

Community   State   Nation

Citizens

Review What You Learned

2. How do people in the United States choose their town leaders?

3. Where does the United States Congress meet?

4. Name two things you can do to be a responsible citizen.

5. What is the Liberty Bell?

Key Words

Use the key words below to complete the sentences.

citizen (p. 206)

government (p. 195)

mayor (p. 196)

monument (p. 212)

pledge (p. 207)

President (p. 202)

6. The _____ is the leader of a city.

7. People who work together to bring order to a community, state, or nation are called a _____ .

8. The _____ is the leader of our country.

9. A _____ is a promise.

10. A person who belongs to a community or a nation is called a _____ .

11. A _____ is a statue or building that reminds people of heroes or past events.

Write a Newspaper Article

12. Suppose you are a reporter for a school newspaper. Write an article about the school rules.

   • What are some of your school rules? What happens if someone breaks them?

   • Are there any new rules you think the school should have?

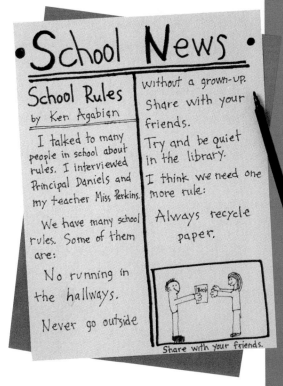

Use the chart to answer these questions.

Monuments and Libraries		
Town Name	Monuments	Libraries
Stockton	3	1
Milford	1	2
Palmer	0	2

13. What is this chart about? Name the columns and the rows.

14. Which town has the fewest libraries?

15. How many monuments does the town of Milford have?

Make a map of your classroom on a separate piece of paper.

16. List the things in your classroom you want to show on your map.

17. Create a symbol for everything you want to show.

18. Now draw your map with a key. Are all the symbols drawn in the right places?

My America Poster

1. Make a list of things you have learned about government, good citizens, and our nation's symbols.

2. Choose words, symbols, and phrases from your list to put on your poster.

3. Draw pictures or cut out photos from old magazines to show how you feel about living in the United States.

4. Place the pictures near the words they match.

5. Share your poster. Hang it on a bulletin board.

Things You'll Need

- big sheet of paper
- crayons or markers
- paste or glue
- scissors
- magazines, newspapers, photographs of yourself, family, or friends

Read On Your Own

Let's Read Biography:
Abraham Lincoln

Let's Read Biography:
Barbara Jordan

City Green
by DyAnne DiSalvo-Ryan

Atlas

NORTH
AMERICA

UNITED STATES

*ATLANTIC
OCEAN*

*PACIFIC
OCEAN*

SOUTH
AMERICA

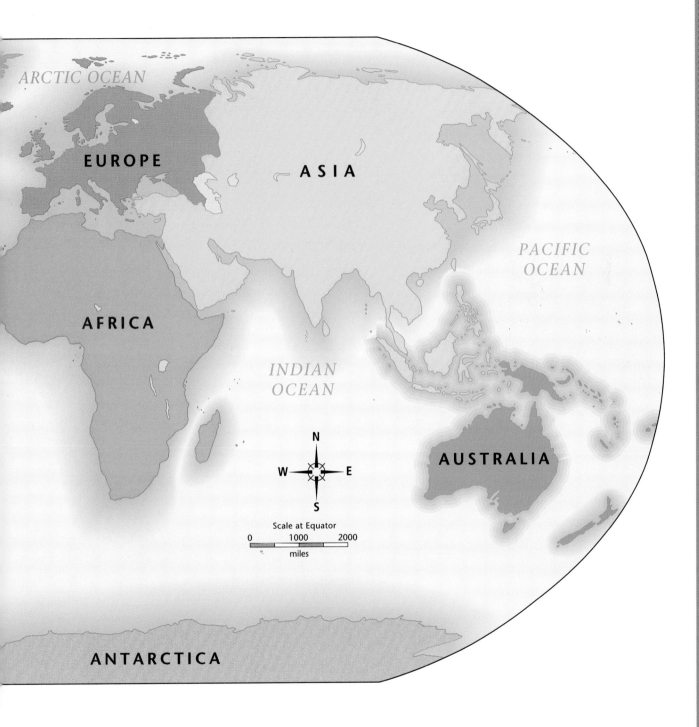

ARCTIC OCEAN

EUROPE

ASIA

PACIFIC
OCEAN

AFRICA

INDIAN
OCEAN

N
W ✦ E
S

AUSTRALIA

Scale at Equator
0   1000   2000
miles

ANTARCTICA

ARCTIC OCEAN

PACIFIC
OCEAN

HAWAII

N
W   E
S

miles 0   400   800

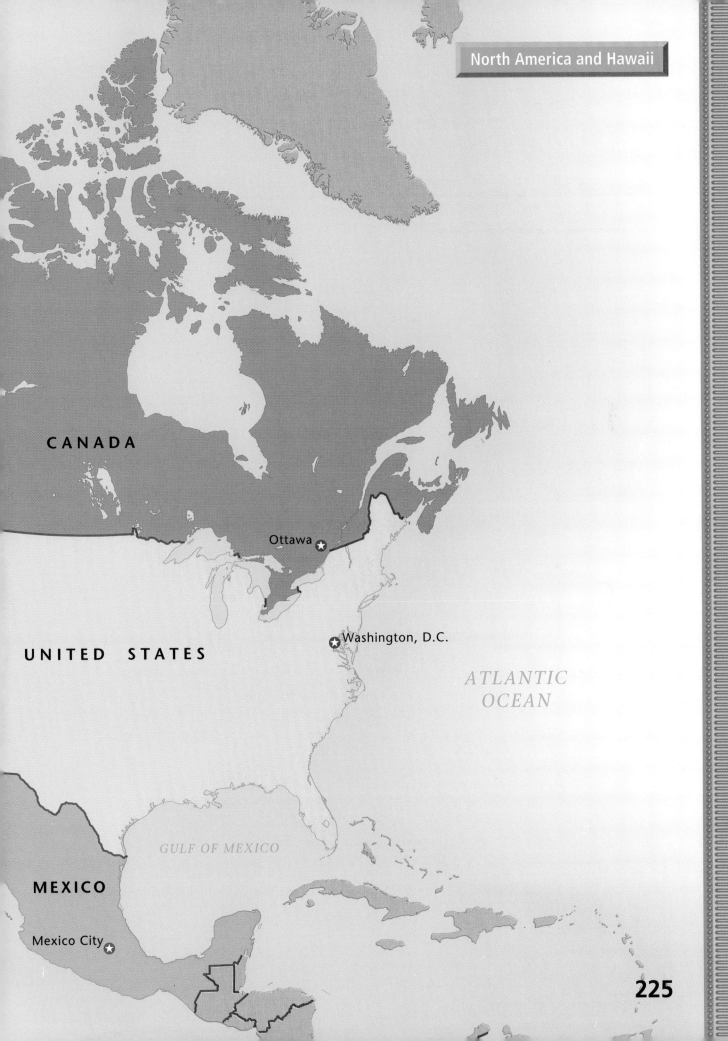

CANADA

Ottawa ★

UNITED STATES

Washington, D.C. ★

ATLANTIC
OCEAN

GULF OF MEXICO

MEXICO

Mexico City ★

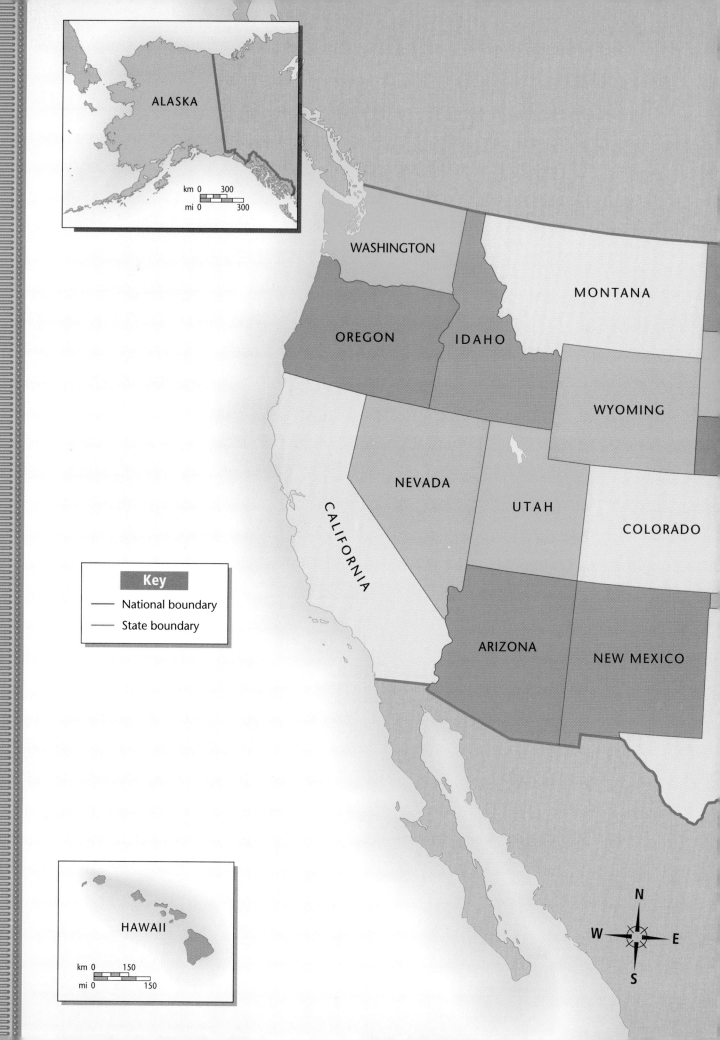

ALASKA

km 0   300
mi 0   300

WASHINGTON

MONTANA

OREGON   IDAHO

WYOMING

NEVADA

UTAH

COLORADO

CALIFORNIA

ARIZONA   NEW MEXICO

Key
—— National boundary
—— State boundary

HAWAII

km 0   150
mi 0   150

N
W   E
S

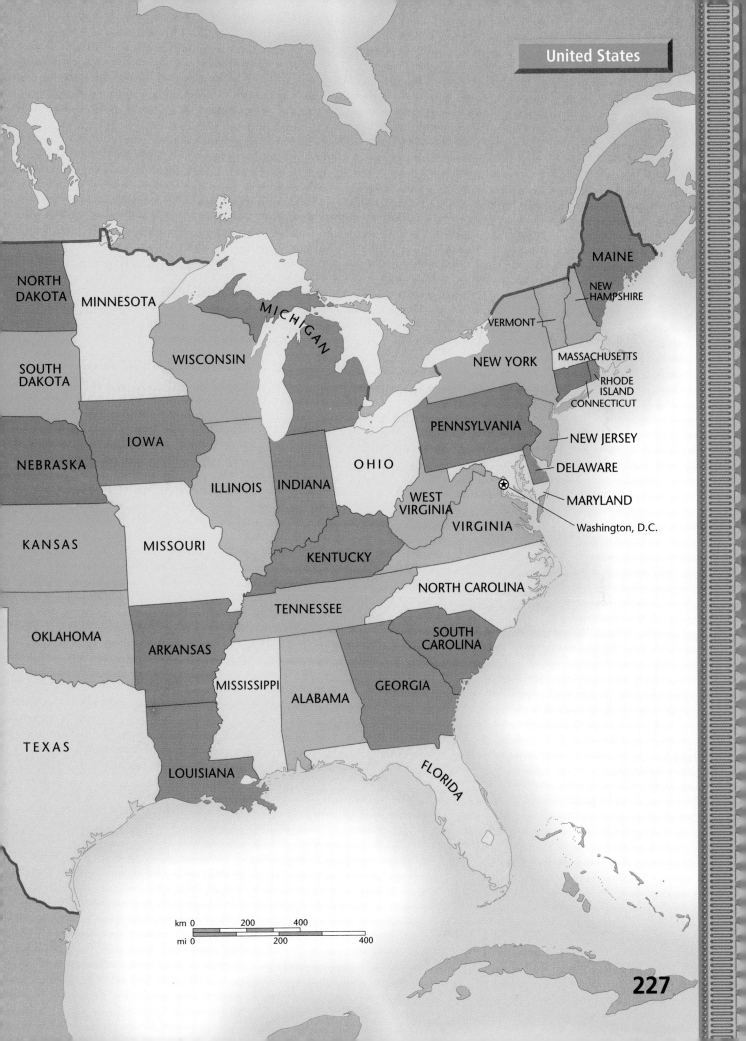

MAINE

NEW HAMPSHIRE

VERMONT

MASSACHUSETTS

RHODE ISLAND

CONNECTICUT

NEW JERSEY

DELAWARE

MARYLAND

Washington, D.C.

NORTH DAKOTA

MINNESOTA

MICHIGAN

WISCONSIN

NEW YORK

SOUTH DAKOTA

PENNSYLVANIA

IOWA

OHIO

NEBRASKA

ILLINOIS

INDIANA

WEST VIRGINIA

VIRGINIA

KANSAS

MISSOURI

KENTUCKY

NORTH CAROLINA

TENNESSEE

OKLAHOMA

ARKANSAS

SOUTH CAROLINA

MISSISSIPPI

ALABAMA

GEORGIA

TEXAS

LOUISIANA

FLORIDA

km 0   200   400

mi 0   200   400

Geographic Glossary

1 coast
the land next to the ocean

▼ desert
a dry area where few plants grow

2 forest
a large area of land where many trees grow

harbor
a protected body of water where ships can safely stop

hill
a raised mass of land, smaller than a mountain

island
a body of land with water all around it

lake
a body of water with land all around it

3 mountain
a steep mass of land, much higher than the surrounding country

4 ocean
a salty body of water covering a large area of the earth

▼ plain
a broad, flat area of land

river
a large stream of water that runs into a lake, ocean, or another river

▲ valley
low land between hills or mountains

229

Glossary

A . . . .

agriculture

The raising of plants or animals for food. (p. 35)
Growing corn or raising cattle is part of **agriculture**.

ancestor

Someone in your family who lived before you were born. (p. 164)
Your great-grandfather is an **ancestor**.

B . . . .

beliefs

Ideas that people think are true. (p. 71)
During Hanukkah Jews show their **beliefs** through a special ceremony.

C . . . .

citizen

A person who belongs to a community or a country. (p. 206)
An American **citizen** needs a passport to visit other countries.

city

A community where many people live and work close together. (p. 22)
There are tall buildings in a **city**.

city council

A group of people who help the mayor run the government. (p. 196)
The **city council** meets once a week at city hall.

colonist

A person who lives in a colony. (p. 130)
Colonists settled in Plymouth, Massachusetts.

colony

A place that is ruled by another country. (p. 130)
South Carolina was once a **colony** ruled by Great Britain.

community

A place where a group of people live, work, and follow the same rules and laws. (p. 16)
The **community** has a busy main street.

Congress

The group of people in the national government who make and change laws. (p. 202)
Congress meets at the Capitol building in Washington, D.C.

consumer

Someone who buys or uses goods or services. (p. 99)
The **consumer** is buying crayons.

continent
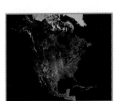
A very large body of land. (p. 55)
You live on the **continent** of North America.

contribution

Something you do or give that helps people in need or makes places better for others. (p. 178)
Jonas Salk made a **contribution** when he found a cure for polio.

country

The land and the people who share the same laws and have the same leader. Another word for nation. (p. 53)
The United States is a **country** in North America.

culture

The way of life of a group of people including, a shared past, beliefs, art, music, folktales, clothing, language, and food. (p. 71)
One way that people show their **culture** is through their art.

crop

A plant a farmer grows to gather. (p. 65)
The farmer planted a huge **crop** of corn.

E . . . .

election

A time when people vote to choose their leaders. (p. 195)

Jill votes for a club president in the **election**.

explorer

A person who travels to learn new things. (p. 126)

Christopher Columbus was an **explorer**.

export

To sell and send goods to other countries. (p. 107)

Companies **export** their products.

F . . . .

factory

A building where people work to make goods. (p. 94)

Yo-yos are made in a **factory**.

freedom

Being able to act and make decisions for yourself. (p. 136)

The Statue of Liberty is a symbol of **freedom**.

G . . . .

goods

The things that people make or grow to sell. (p. 94)

Socks are **goods**.

government

A group of people who work together to bring order to a community, state, or nation. (p. 195)

The President is the leader of the United States **government**.

governor

The leader of a state. (p. 197)

The **governor** visited the classroom.

group

A number of people who work, live, or spend time together. (p. 10)

A club is one kind of **group**.

H . . . .

hero

A person who does something very special to help others. (p. 178)

George Washington is a **hero**.

history

The story of the past and the people who came before us. (p. 122)
Our families have a **history**.

holiday

A day that honors a person or a special event. (p. 175)
Thanksgiving is a national **holiday**.

honor

To show special attention or respect to someone or something. (p. 123)
We **honor** the best spellers.

I . . . .

immigrant

A person who moves from one country to another. (p. 150)
My grandmother is an **immigrant**.

import

To buy goods and services from other countries. (p. 108)
The United States plans to **import** bananas from countries in Central America.

income

The money people earn. (p. 89)
A family's **income** pays for food, clothing, and shelter.

island

Land with water all around it. (p.47)
We crossed the bridge to get to the **island**.

J . . . .

job

The work that someone does to earn an income. (p. 93)
A firefighter has an important **job**.

judge

A person who makes important decisions in a court of law. (p. 203)
A **judge** works in a courtroom.

L . . . .

lake

A body of water with land all around it. (p. 48)
Row the boat on the **lake**.

language

The words that people speak, read, and write. (p. 73)

Many people use sign **language**.

law

A community rule that people agree to obey. (p. 16)

A court decides if a **law** is fair.

M . . . .

manufacture

To make something. (p. 98)

The factory will **manufacture** crayons.

mayor

The leader of a city or a town. (p. 196)

The **mayor** met with our class leaders.

monument

A statue or a building that is built to remind people of heroes or important events. (p. 212)
That **monument** honors George Washington.

mountain

High, steep land that rises above the ground. (p. 46)

We climbed a high **mountain** on Sunday.

N . . . .

nation

The land and the people who share the same laws, and

have the same leader. Another word for country. (p. 53)
Every **nation** has its own flag.

natural resource

Something from nature that people

use. Some of these are air, soil, trees, rocks, plants, water, and oil. (p. 59)
Trees are a **natural resource**.

needs

Things that people must have to live. All people need

food, clothing, and shelter. (p. 87)
Food is one of three basic **needs**.

neighborhood

The area around your home. (p. 17)

Our school is an important part of our **neighborhood**.

O . . . .

ocean

A large body of salt water. Oceans cover most of the earth. (p. 49)

The Pacific Ocean is the largest **ocean** in the world.

P . . . .

pioneer

Someone who does something first and leads the way for other people. (p. 143)

The **pioneer** traveled in a covered wagon to her new home.

plain

Flat land. (p. 45)

A **plain** can be a good place for farming.

pledge

A promise. (p. 206)

Many people say the **Pledge** of Allegiance in school.

President

The leader of a country or nation. (p. 202)

Abraham Lincoln was our sixteenth **President**.

price

The amount of money consumers pay for goods and services. (p. 102)

The **price** of the yo-yo is 98 cents.

producer

A person who makes or grows something. (p. 98)

The farmer was a **producer** of fresh fruit.

R . . . .

region

An area of land with features that are alike, such as natural resources, landforms, or weather. (p. 64)

The South is a **region** of the United States.

relative

A person who is part of the same family today. (p. 164)
Her grandmother is her favorite **relative**.

responsibility

Something that you should do. (p. 208)
Caring for the earth is your **responsibility**.

river

A long, moving, body of fresh water that flows into lakes, oceans, or other rivers. (p. 49)
The **river** flows through the state forest.

rule

A statement that tells what people may or may not do. (p. 11)
Each student listed a **rule** for our class.

rural

A word used to describe the countryside. (p. 34)
Many people in **rural** communities live in small towns.

S . . . .

service

A job that helps other people. (p. 95)
Mail carriers provide an important **service**.

settler

A person who moves to a new place and makes a home. (p. 128)
The **settler** built a house.

shelter

Something that protects or covers. (p. 88)
A house is one kind of **shelter**.

slavery

A cruel, unfair system in which one person was forced to work for another without pay. (p. 148)
During the Civil War, the United States fought over **slavery**.

social studies

The study of how and where people live, the rules they make, and the stories of their past. (p. 11)
This is our **social studies** book.

state

A smaller place that is part of our country. (p. 54)

Florida is one **state** in the United States.

Supreme Court

The nine judges who decide if laws in the United States are fair. (p. 202)

The judges on the **Supreme Court** keep their jobs for life.

suburb

A community near a city. (p. 28)

There are many houses in my **suburb**.

T . . . .

tax

Money charged by a country or town to help pay for schools, roads, and other things. (p. 136)

On April 15 people must pay their income **tax.**

tradition

An idea, custom, or belief that parents pass down to their children. (p. 174)

The Fourth of July parade is a **tradition** in our town.

transportation

Any way of moving things or people from one place to another. (p. 24)

A bus is a kind of **transportation**.

U . . . .

urban

A word used to describe a city. (p. 22)

An **urban** community usually has many people and buildings.

V . . . .

valley

The land between mountains or hills. (p. 46)

My house is in a **valley**.

vote

To make a choice. (p.139)

The children can **vote** for their favorite hero.

Index

Page numbers with *m* before them refer to maps. Page numbers with *p* refer to pictures. Page numbers with *c* refer to charts.

Firefighters

Natural Resources

Credits

Acknowledgments

For each of the selections listed below, grateful acknowledgment is made for permission to excerpt and/or reprint original or copyrighted material, as follows:

Permissioned Material

From *50 Simple Things Kids Can Do To Save The Earth*, by The EarthWorks Group. Copyright © 1990 by John Javna. Reprinted by permission of Andrews and McMeel. All rights reserved.

"The House I Live In," words by Lewis Allan. Copyright 1942 by Chappell & Co. © Renewed. All rights reserved. Used by permission of Warner Bros. Publications U.S. Inc., Miami, FL 33014.

"La Libertad"/"Liberty," by A.L. Jauregui, translated by Angela de Hoyos from *Gallito de Plata* by A.L. Jauregui. Translation copyright © 1974 by Angela de Hoyos. Reprinted by permission of Editorial Avante, S.A.

"Minnie," from *Move Over, Mother Goose!* by Ruth I. Dowell. Copyright © 1987 by Gryphon House, Inc., P.O. Box 207, Beltsville, MD 20704-0207. l.800.638.0928. Reprinted with permission from Gryphon House, Inc.

"My People," from *Collected Poems* by Langston Hughes. Copyright © 1994 by the Estate of Langston Hughes. Reprinted by permission of Alfred A. Knopf Inc.

From "My Words Are Tied in One," from a Yokuts prayer, translated by A.L. Kroeber in *Handbook of the Indians of California*, by A.L. Kroeber, published in Bulletin 78 in 1925 by the Bureau of American Ethnology (B.A.E.) and the Smithsonian Institution.

"Our Block," from *CITY POEMS* by Lois Lenski. Copyright © 1954, 1956, 1965, 1971 by Lois Lenski. Reprinted by permission of Steven Covey, son of Lois Lenski.

"Our Family Comes from 'Round the World," from *Fathers, Mothers, Sisters, Brothers* by Mary Ann Hoberman, illustrated by Marilyn Hafner. Text copyright © 1991 by Mary Ann Hoberman. Illustrations copyright © 1991 by Marilyn Hafner. Reprinted by permission of Little, Brown and Company Inc.

"Roll On, Columbia," words by Woody Guthrie, music based on *GOODNIGHT, IRENE* by Huddie Ledbetter and John A. Lomax. TRO -©- Copyright 1936 (Renewed), 1957 (Renewed), and 1963 (Renewed) Ludlow Music, Inc., New York, NY. Used by permission.

"Sweet Job: Kids in Business," from *National Geographic World* magazine, February 1991. Copyright © 1991 by National Geographic World. *World* is the official magazine for Junior Members of the National Geographic Society. Reprinted by permission.

"When I First Came to This Land," words and music by Oscar Brand. TRO - Copyright © 1957 (Renewed), 1965 (Renewed) Ludlow Music, Inc., New York, NY. Used by permission.

Photo Credits

cover Bill Losh/FPG Int. (inset) Corbis/Bettmann. **title page spread** (background) Donovan Reese/Tony Stone Images. Eric Horan/Index Stock. **vii** Patrick Bennett/Corbis. **viii** Vince Streano/Corbis. **ix** The Granger Collection. **xiii** (l) Laurie Bayer/International Stock. Mark Tomalty/Masterfile. **8** Sandy Felsenthal/Corbis. **8-9** Tom and Dee Ann McCarthy/The Stock Market. **9** (l) Bruce Stoddard/FPG. (m) Tom Benoit/Tony Stone Images. (r) Kunio Owaki/The Stock Market. **11** Richard T. Nowitz/Corbis. **15** Myrleen Ferguson/Photo Edit. **17** Sandy Felsenthal/Corbis. **20** Christie's Images/Superstock. **21** E.R.I.M./Tony Stone Images. **22** Superstock. **23** (t) Bruce Stoddard 1996/FPG. (b) Rich LaSalle/Tony Stone Images. **24** Joseph Sohm, ChromoSohm Inc./Corbis. **25** Oklahoma City Convention and Visitors Bureau. **27** Jean Pragen/Tony Stone Images. **28** (l) Randy Wells/Tony Stone Images. (r) Joseph Sohm, ChromoSohm, Inc./Corbis. **29** Tom Benoit/Tony Stone Images. **30** (t) Martin Rogers/Woodfin Camp and Associates/PNI. Courtesy of the Perez family. **31** Kunio Owaki/The Stock Market. **35** Ric Ergenbright Photography. **42** (l) Mark Segal/Tony Stone Images. (m) Patrick Bennett/Corbis. **42-43** David Muench Photography. **43** (l) Walter Hodges/Westlight. (r) Bob Daemmrich/Stock Boston. **44** (l) Phil Schermeister/Corbis. (r) Bob Daemmrich/Stock Boston/PNI. **45** Gary Irving/Tony Stone Images. **46** (l) Mark Segal/Tony Stone Images. (r) Nicholas deVore III/Photographers Aspen/PNI. **47** (t) Wayne Eastep/Tony Stone Images. (b) Patrick Bennett/Corbis. **48** Yann Arthus-Bertrand/Corbis. **49** Larry Ulrich/Tony Stone Images. **54** Superstock. **58** Robert Brenner/Photo Edit. **59** (t) Tony Freeman/Photo Edit. (l) Grantpix/Photo Researchers. (r) Phil Schofield/Tony Stone Images. **60** Grant Heilman Photography. **61** (t) Walter Hodges/Westlight. (b) Montes De Oca, Art 1997/FPG. **63** Phil Schermeister/Corbis. **65** (t) David R. Frazier Photography. (b) Bill Gillette/Stock Boston. **66** (t) Dean Abramson/Stock Boston. (b) Grant Heilman Photography. **71** (t) Associated Press/Calgary Herald-Shannon Oatway. (b) Bob Daemmrich/Stock Boston. **72** (t) Bill Brooks/Masterfile. (b) PhotoDisc. **72-73** Alec Pytlowany/Masterfile. **73** (t) Chris Aveno/AlaskaStock. (b) The Purcell Team/Corbis. **74** (t) Jacksonville Museum of Contemporary Art, Florida/Superstock. (b) G. Dagli Orti. **75** Danny Lehman/Corbis. **84** Michael Newman/Photo Edit/PNI. **85** (l) Courtesy of Binney and Smith. (r) Lester Lefkowitz/The Stock Market. **88** (t) Bob Daemmrich Photo, Inc. (b) 1997 Chris Arend/AlaskaStock. **90** Courtesy of Karen Nicksitch. **92** (l) Richard Hutchings/Photo Edit. (m) Michael Newman/Photo Edit/PNI. (r) Vince Streano/Corbis. **93** NASA. **94** Dick Luria/FPG. **95** Ed Bock/The Stock Market. **97** David Young-Wolf/Photo Edit. **98** Courtesy of Binney and Smith. Crayola, chevron and serpentine designs are registered trademarks; rainbow/swash design is a trademark of Binney & Smith, used with permission. **100** (t) Courtesy of Binney and Smith. (b) Peter Gridley 1997/FPG. **101** Courtesy of Binney and Smith. **102** Courtesy of Binney and Smith. **107** Lester Lefkowitz/The Stock Market. **109** (t) Jim Winkley/Eye Ubiquitous/Corbis. (b) George Hall/Corbis. **112** Martin Harvey/The Wildlife Collection. **113** Jackie Bell/National Geographic Society. **114** Paul Gero/National Geographic Society. **115** Kevin Horan/National Geographic Society. **120** (l) John Running Photography. (m) Metropolitan Museum of Art, New York City/Superstock. (r) Kindra Clineff. **120-121** Associated Press/Liz Schultz. **121** (m) Rick Egan. (r) Corbis/Bettmann. **122** John Running Photography. **123** Lee Boltin Library. **124** (l) Runk/Schoenberger/Grant Heilman. (r) Native American Archives of The Museum, Colquitt, GE. **125** BC Archives. **127** Superstock. **128** George H.H. Huey. **129** Dave G. Houser/Corbis. **130** Kindra Clineff. **133** Koni Nordmann/Contact Press Images/PNI. **135** (l) Colonial Williamsburg. (r) The Granger Collection. **136** Colonial Williamsburg. **137** Dave G. Houser/Corbis. **138** The Purcell Team/Corbis. **139** (t) Corbis/Bettmann. (b) Ted Spiegel. **141** Corbis. **143** (t) Division of Political History, Smithsonian Institution, Washington, D.C. (b) Rick Egan. **144** Corbis/Bettmann. **148** Corbis/Bettmann. **149** Corbis. **150** (t) Corbis/Bettmann. (b) National Park Service, Statue of Liberty, Ellis Island National Monument. **151** Corbis. **152** Corbis. **153** Jose L. Pelaez/The Stock Market. **154** (l) Laurie Bayer/International Stock. (r) Mark Tomalty/Masterfile. **162** Bob Daemmrich Photo, Inc. **162-163** Tom and DeeAnn McCarthy/The Stock Market. **163** (l) Phil Schermeister/Corbis. (m) Associated Press/F.J. Flynn. (r) Corbis/Bettmann. **165** Richard T. Nowitz/Corbis. **166** Courtesy of the Hoogendoorn family. **167** Courtesy of the Lee family. **171** (l) David Young-Wolf/Tony Stone Images. (r) Ariel Skelley/The Stock Market. (r) Indexstock. **174** Bob Daemmrich Photo Inc. **175** (l) Patrick Ramsey/International Stock. (m) Annie Griffiths-Belt/Corbis. (r) Phil Schermeister/Corbis. **176** (t) Courtesy of the Pendleton District Commission. (b) John Elk/Tony Stone Images. **181** (t) Corbis/Bettmann. (m) Associated Press/F.J. Flynn. (b) Associated Press. **182** (t) Gianni Dagli Orti/Corbis. (b) "The Seattle Art Museum," Gift of Friends of the Seattle Art Museum in honor of the 75th birthday of Dr. Richard E. Fuller. Photo by Paul Macapia. **183** Corbis/Bettmann. **192** (l) Alan Schein/The Stock Market. (m) Will Van Overbeek. **192-193** Craig Aurness/Corbis. **193** (l) Mug Shots/The Stock Market. (m) Lawrence Migdale. (r) Joseph Sohm, ChromoSohm Inc./Corbis. **197** Courtesy of the Office of the Governor of South Carolina, photo by Travis Bell, State Photographer. **200** Corbis/Bettmann. **201** PhotoDisc. **202** (t) Miles Ertman/Masterfile. (b) Alan Schein/The Stock Market. **203** Miles Ertman/Masterfile. **205** Jim Pickerell/Nonstock, Inc./PNI. **206** Elliot Varner Smith/International Stock. **207** Lawrence Migdale. **208** Myrleen Ferguson/Photo Edit. **209** Yann Arthus-Bertrand/Corbis. **210** Superstock. **212** (l) Kelly-Mooney Photography/Corbis. (r) Joseph Nettis/Tony Stone Images. **213** (t) Corbis. (b) Joseph Sohm, ChromoSohm Inc./Corbis. **215** Courtesy of the Nashua River Watershed Archives. **217** Bokelburg/The Image Bank. **228** David Muench/Corbis. **228-229** James Schwabel/Panoramic Images. **229** (l) Gary Irving/Tony Stone Images. (r) Bryan Pickering/Corbis. **230** (agriculture) Larry Lefever/Grant Heilman. (ancestor) Corbis/Bettmann. (beliefs) Richard Hutchings/Photo Edit. (citizen) PhotoDisc. (city) Tom Pix/Peter Arnold Inc. (city council) Nancy Sheehan/Photo Edit. (colonist) Kindra Klineff. **231** (community) Stephen Marks/Stock Photos. (congress) Don Carl Steffen/Photo Researchers. (continent) E.R.I.M./Tony Stone Images. (contribution) Corbis/Bettmann. (culture) Superstock. (crop) Larry Lefever/Grant Heilman Photography, Inc. **232** (explorer) Superstock. (export) Lester Lefkowitz/The Stock Market. (freedom) PhotoDisc. (government) Eddie Hironaka/The Image Bank. (governor) Office of the Governor of the State of South Carolina, photo by Travis Bell, State Photographer. (hero) Corbis/Bettmann. **233** (history) John Running. (holiday) Ted Curtain for © Plimoth Plantation. (honor) Charles Gupton/Stock Boston. (immigrant) Corbis/Bettmann. (import) Danny Lehman/Corbis. (income) Icon Communications/FPG Int. (island) Wayne Eastep/Tony Stone Images. (job) Grantpix/Photo Researchers. (judge) Bob Daemmrich/Stock Boston. (lake) Yann Arthus-Bertrand/Corbis. **234** (law) Jay Freis/The Image Bank. (manufacture) Courtesy of Binney and Smith. (mayor) David Witbeck/Mercury Pictures. (monument) Joseph Sohm, ChromoSohm Inc./Corbis. (mountain) Mark Segal/Tony Stone Images. (nation) Paul Almasy/Corbis. (natural resource) Grant Heilman Photography Inc. **235** (ocean) Peter French/Bruce Coleman, Inc. (pioneer) Rick Egan. (plain) Gary Irving/Tony Stone Images. (president) Library of Congress. (producer) Dick Luria/FPG Int. **236** (relative) Spencer Grant/Photo Edit. (river) Larry Ulrich/Tony Stone Images. (rural) Brian Yarvin/Peter Arnold Inc. (services) Bill Losh/FPG Int. (settler) Archive Photos/PNI. (shelter) Sandy Felsenthal/Corbis. **237** (supreme court) Photographed by Richard Strauss, Smithsonian Institution/Collection, The Supreme Court Historical Society. (suburb) Tom Benoit/Tony Stone Images. (tax) Murray Alcosser/The Image Bank. (tradition) Firefly Productions/The Stock Market. (transportation) Andre Jenny/Stock South/PNI. (urban) Barrie Rokeach. (valley) Nicholas deVore III/Photographers Aspen/PNI.

Assignment Photo Credits

vi (b), **8** (bm), **11** (t), **12, 13** (t), **16, 236** (rule) Tracy Aiguier; **126, 162** (bm), **164, 184, 221** Joel Benjamin; **8** (bl), **10, 13** (l) Cheryl Clegg; **64** Kindra Clineff; **94** (m) Dave Derkacy; **84-85, 85** (bm), **99, 231** (consumer) Scott Goodwin; **viii, 84** (bl), **86, 87, 91, 93** (b), **110, 234** (needs) Kimberly Holcombe; **x** (b), **22** (r), **52** (l), **121** (bl), **161, 168, 180, 194, 195, 196, 211, 232** (group), **237** (vote) Tony Scarpetta

Map Credits

Map Quest. com Inc: **24, 31, 43, 50, 51, 53, 54, 65, 70, 77, 82, 108, 124, 136, 146, 147, 149, 160, 222-227**; Ortelius Design: **18, 19, 33, 40**; XNR Productions, Inc.: **127, 142**.

Illustration Credits

JoAnn Adinolfi: **37**; Tim Coffey: **156-157**; Nenad Jakesevic: **130-131, 132, 134-135**; Rob Schuster: **105**; Marina Thompson: **38**; Will Williams: **26, 96, 128-129**; Ashley Wolff: **79**